# Probing Understanding

We dedicate this book to Roger Osborne, who did so much to encourage us and many others to explore and promote students' understanding. His untimely death in 1985 deprived Education of one of its most delightful personalities.

# Probing Understanding

Richard White and Richard Gunstone

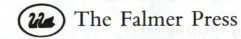

The Falmer Press

(A member of the Taylor & Francis Group)
London ● New York ● Philadelphia

UK      The Falmer Press, 4 John St., London, WC1N 2ET
USA     The Falmer Press, Taylor & Francis Inc., 1900 Frost Road, Suite 101,
        Bristol, PA 19007

First published 1992

**A catalogue record for this book is available
from the British Library**

**Library of Congress-in-Publication Data are available
on request**

ISBN 0 75070 047 5 cased
ISBN 0 75070 048 3

Jacket design by Caroline Archer

Typeset in 11/13 Bembo by
Graphicraft Typesetters Ltd, Hong Kong

*Printed in Great Britain by Burgess Science Press, Basingstoke*

# Contents

# Acknowledgments

We owe much to the teachers who have used and told us about the probes of understanding that we describe here, and to the students with whom we tried them ourselves. Their participation gives our account whatever credibility it possesses.

Cath Henderson, Sandra Bosmans and Claude Sironi helped us with the mechanical production of the manuscript. Mechanical does not imply trivial. The professionalism of their work made it possible for us to do our own work better.

Individually we record appreciation of each other's part. This book marks another step in a long, productive and entirely enjoyable friendship. The order of our names bears no connotation of difference in contribution. This is an equal, as well as equable, partnership.

# Preface

In Lewis Carroll's great nonsense poem, *The Hunting of the Snark*, unlikely characters set forth to capture a dangerous and unseen beast. Their implements are unlikely, too:

> They sought it with thimbles, they sought it with care;
> They pursued it with forks and hope;
> They threatened its life with a railway-share;
> They charmed it with smiles and soap.

Like the Snark, understanding is an elusive quarry. Teachers and students want to secure it, but how can they do so, and how will they know when they have succeeded? Like the Snark hunters, we believe that there is a much better chance when a variety of methods, though more rational than theirs, is employed.

We contend that assessment in schools is too often narrow in range. The oral questions that teachers ask in class and their informal and formal written tests usually are confined to requiring short answers of a word or two or a number, a choice from a few alternatives, or 'essays' of various lengths. While there is nothing wrong with these tests, they are limited in type. Limited tests provide a limited measure of understanding, and, worse, promote limited understanding. We advocate use of diverse probes of understanding as an effective means of promoting high quality learning.

Our purpose in this book is to provide teachers, at all levels of education and of all subjects, with a greater range of practical methods of probing their students' understanding.

Some of the probes were first used in research studies; the word association procedure is an instance. Others, such as the fortune line, teachers invented for their own purposes. And others, such as relational diagrams, were ideas which, if not inventions of our own, we saw as useful in probing understanding. We have used nearly all of them in our own teaching. As well as that direct experience, we have reports from other teachers on their experiences with them. Thus these are not abstract notions, but procedures that have been tried in the classroom.

Each procedure illuminates a particular facet of understanding. None is better than another, or than currently popular methods; they just do different things. It is their diversity that empowers the teacher, and that directs the student to learning with deeper understanding.

Each chapter follows the same sequence. First there is a brief description of the probe, which includes a single sentence statement of its use and an example. A more extensive discussion of the purpose follows. Next there is step-by-step listing of the procedure, and numerous examples. Nearly all of the examples are from actual classroom use, though sometimes we have re-drawn students' productions because they were faint or in handwriting difficult to read, and in a few instances we invented an example when we did not have a real one ready to hand. We are conscious that there is a greater proportion of examples from science than other subjects, a consequence of our own experience in secondary school teaching and because researchers in understanding have been most active in science learning. Nevertheless, we believe that there is enough here of value for teachers of all subjects at all levels of education.

The examples precede advice on how to introduce the probe to students. Users of a new probe should not expect it to work perfectly first time. Not only must the user become more skilled, but the students have to learn how to respond. That takes time and practice. The advice is intended to make the first encounter successful. Once teacher and students are familiar with the procedure, they might find it productive to explore variations and extensions, so we describe next some possibilities — which by no means exhaust the range of what might be done. Then there is a discussion of what the probe reveals about understanding.

We set out procedures for scoring students' responses, though we often express reservations about the effect of converting the rich information the probes discover to a single number or letter grade. The chapters end with implications the probe has for teaching, and details of further reading.

We do not present the probes as a comprehensive list. Rather we hope they will be seen as no more than a starting set that will stimulate the invention and widespread use of many more imaginative and powerful ways of assessing understanding. For we are convinced that the more probes that teachers use, the sounder their appreciation of their students' understanding, the more interesting they and their students will find their teaching, and the better will be the learning that follows.

*Richard T. White*
and
*Richard F. Gunstone,*
June 1991

Chapter 1

# The Nature of Understanding

'What are you learning?' asked the visitor to the classroom. 'Not much', replied the 14-year-old student. 'Right now I have to understand South America'.

Presumably the student's teacher told her that understanding South America was what she had to do, but what does it mean? What is involved in understanding South America, or the French Revolution or quadratic equations or acids and bases or musical notation or impressionist painting or Japanese grammar? And how could one test whether a student understands these things?

It is important to answer these questions, since almost every statement of aims for education, whether addressed to a whole school system, a single year of education, a subject syllabus, or even a single lesson, now includes understanding as an important outcome, a higher form of learning than rote acquisition of knowledge. It was not always so, as a comparison of present–day and 1930s school tests or content-specific tests described in the Mental Measurements Yearbooks (e.g., Buros, 1938), will show. The tests of fifty years ago are largely measures of ability to recall facts or to apply standard algorithms, while those of today more commonly make an effort to see whether the knowledge can be used to solve novel problems. The publication of the well-known taxonomy of educational objectives (Bloom, 1956) both reflected and spurred the widespread acceptance, thirty years ago, of the need to promote understanding. Since then operational definitions of understanding have developed for each school subject, definitions which spread from teacher to teacher through sharing of ideas about tests or through the more effective controls of central examination authorities or textbooks that contain sample questions. Texts even manage to spread ideas so that question styles in a subject are often virtually identical in widely separated countries.

There is nothing wrong with an operational definition of a complex construct like understanding, provided that we recognize that the definition is not the only possible way of measuring it. Restriction of measurement to one form, or too small a number of forms, can distort the construct and lead to neglect of important aspects of it. This, of course, has come to be recognized for another widely-used construct, intelligence, where the Stanford-Binet style of test was dominant for a long time but is now paralleled by different styles such as Raven's progressive matrices and individually-taken tests like the Wechsler Intelligence Scale for Children.

In the case of understanding, a limited definition will have a restricting effect on teaching and learning. In physics, for example, tests of understanding in Australia and America are mainly short problems such as in Figure 1.1; extended explanations of physical phenomena are required rarely. We (Gunstone and White, 1981) found that many first-year university students of physics could not write explanations of simple phenomena such as the acceleration of a falling object, even though they had passed a difficult entry test of one hundred problems. Probably that deficiency resulted from neglecting that aspect of understanding in tests and in teaching. If it were tested, either in an external examination or by the teacher, it would be taught and learned.

Our concern is that when the range of procedures for testing understanding is narrow, the understanding that schools promote is limited and lop-sided. Since we value understanding and believe that there is a direct connection between forms of testing and what is taught and learned, we want to broaden the repertoire of styles of tests that teachers use. That is the purpose of this book.

A limited range of tests promotes limited forms of understanding, while good learning styles should follow from frequent experience with diverse test forms. But are all forms useful? Which should be used for what purpose? What sorts exist? In order to see what possibilities there are for tests beyond those in common use we need to go beyond operational definitions of understanding and describe directly what we take it to mean. Then we can see the limitations of present tests and how they should be supplemented.

We could try to define understanding in a sentence, but a simple definition cannot encompass all the facets of so complex a concept. Indeed we feel that simple definitions are partly responsible for the current limited appreciation of understanding in teaching, learning

A sphere of mass 3 kg travelling North at $2\,\mathrm{m\,s^{-1}}$ collides with another sphere of mass 4 kg travelling East at $2\,\mathrm{m\,s^{-1}}$.

39. The magnitude of their resultant momentum after collision will be:
    A.   zero.
    B.   $2\,\mathrm{kg\,m\,s^{-1}}$,
    C.   $10\,\mathrm{kg\,m\,s^{-1}}$,
    D.   $14\,\mathrm{kg\,m\,s^{-1}}$,
    E.   dependent on whether the collision was elastic or inelastic.

40. The total kinetic energy of the two spheres after collision will be:
    A.   10 J.
    B.   14 J.
    C.   20 J.
    D.   28 J.
    E.   dependent on whether the collision was elastic or inelastic.

Figure 1.1: *Example of problem typically used to measure understanding in physics (from Richard T. White, 1977, Solving Physics Problems, with the permission of the publisher, McGraw-Hill Book Company, Sydney)*

and assessment. An extensive description of understanding is to be preferred.

Part of the difficulty in describing understanding is that the word is applied to a range of targets. People mean rather different things when they say 'I don't understand poetry', 'I don't understand what he said', or 'I don't understand my children'. A first step in describing understanding is to sort out the targets we talk about, and then try to see what lies behind understanding of each.

We find it helpful to specify six targets: understanding of concepts, whole disciplines, single elements of knowledge, extensive communications, situations, and people. We will try to spell out what forms of knowledge lie behind each, before considering what new tests are needed.

## Understanding of Concepts

If you want to know the meaning of a word like *democracy* or *energy*, you can go to a dictionary for a definition of it, but that definition alone is hardly likely to be sufficient for you to feel that you understand the term to any substantial degree. For understanding, you would want to know more about it. That is, to understand a concept you must have in your memory some information about it.

Many theories of learning concentrate on one form of information, that of verbal knowledge or *propositions* (e.g., Ausubel, 1968), but Gagné and White (1978) described a more complete set in which *images, episodes,* and *intellectual skills* complement propositions as elements of memory. To these we would add *strings* and *motor skills* as two further elements that may be relevant to understanding. We need to describe each of these six types of knowledge before we consider how they are involved in understanding of concepts.

Propositions are facts, opinions, or beliefs, such as 'Democracy is the form of government in the United States' or 'There are many forms of energy'. Whether these propositions are correct or not may make little or no difference to the way they are stored in memory or to how they bear on understanding, so we will not distinguish between facts and beliefs. After all, today's fact may be tomorrow's superstition or fallacy. We may believe that the atom's fundamental particles are the proton, neutron, and electron, only to find that a revolution in physics has swept this 'fact' away.

It is, however, worth distinguishing strings from propositions because the two sorts of element are learned and stored differently. Strings are fixed in form, whereas a proposition is an encoding of a meaning where although the meaning is fixed the form of representation is plastic. Thus the two earlier examples could be represented as 'The United States is a democracy' and 'Energy has many forms' without changing the proposition. Such a change in form does not happen with a string such as the Gettysburg address or the Lord's Prayer. Although both the address and the prayer can be expressed in other ways, the typical way of storing them is as strings, unvarying forms. Other examples of strings are proverbs, multiplication tables, scientific laws, mnemonics, and poems.

Images are mental representations of sensory perceptions, which are often visual but can be related to any of the senses. Examples are the mental picture of a voting paper or the feel of 'springiness' in a plunger compressing air in a pump.

Episodes are memories of events that you think happened to you or that you witnessed, such as the recollection of voting in the last election or of doing an experiment to measure the energy released when a quantity of fuel is burned.

Intellectual skills are capacities to carry out classes of tasks, such as being able to vote validly in a preferential system or being able to substitute values in a formula such as $KE = \frac{1}{2} mv^2$. They are memories of procedures. It is important to distinguish between the verbal statement of the procedure and the capacity to perform it. If someone asks you how to distinguish cats from dogs your answer will consist of verbal knowledge, propositions, which you could possess without actually being able to use them to tell cats from dogs. Being able to distinguish the two is the intellectual skill. Alternatively, you might be able to perform the skill without being able to describe how you do it. It is much the same with motor skills. They, too, are capacities to perform classes of tasks, but physical ones rather than mental. Examples are being able to work a voting machine or to wind up a clock. Again, the skill of being able to perform the task is a different form of knowledge from the propositions that describe how it is done. Anyone who doubts that should try to write a description of how to ride a bicycle.

In addition to the six types of knowledge that we have just described, we find it helpful to think of a seventh, more general type called *cognitive strategies*. Cognitive strategies are broad skills used in thinking and learning, such as being able to maintain attention to the task in hand, deducing and inducing, perceiving ambiguities, sorting out relevant from irrelevant information, determining a purpose, and so on. Unlike the other six forms we have described, they are not subject-specific. All of the others tell you something about a particular concept, while cognitive strategies are more to do with general ways of thinking. They will turn out to be important when we consider how understanding is developed, but in considering what we mean by understanding of a concept we will restrict our discussion to the other six types of knowledge.

Our definition of a person's understanding of democracy is that it is the set of propositions, strings, images, episodes, and intellectual and motor skills that the person associates with the label 'democracy'. The richer this set, the better its separate elements are linked with each other, and the clearer each element is formulated, then the greater the understanding.

If the definition were left at that point it would imply that as long as two people had the same amount of knowledge about a topic, equally clear and similarly inter-linked, their understandings would be the same. This would not be sensible, since the details of what they know must affect their understandings. The elements of one person's knowledge may be far more central, more important, than those of the other. Yet it is not easy to say which elements matter. It is doubtful even whether any particular element can be specified as essential to understanding. A definition of the concept may be important, yet concepts can be understood without knowing the definition. Young children, for instance, can have a reasonable understanding of a concept like 'mushroom' without being able to define it. A string such as 'Democracy is government of the people, by the people, for the people' may be part of an understanding of democracy, but can hardly be asserted to be essential to it. Also, people will differ in the value they place on such a string as a contributor to understanding.

The foregoing points show that it is not easy to rate a person's understanding and give it a summary value. One person may know more about democracy than another, but unless the second person's knowledge is a subset of the first's it is not certain that the first has the better understanding. The few things that the second person knows that the first does not may be quite important contributors to understanding. Even if the first person does know all that the other does and more, we would have to consider whether the extra knowledge adds to or subtracts from understanding.

Several points emerge from this discussion. The first is that understanding of a concept is not a dichotomous state, but a continuum. Language traps us here, because we say 'I understand it' or 'He does not understand' when we really mean the level of understanding is above or below some arbitrarily set degree. Everyone understands to some degree anything they know something about. It also follows that understanding is never complete; for we can always add more knowledge, another episode, say, or refine an image, or see new links between things we know already. Even to think in terms of degree or level of understanding can be misleading, because it implies that the construct is unidimensional when the discussion about whether one person understands better than another shows that it is multi-dimensional. I may know more about democracy than you, but your knowledge is sharper, more precise; I may have more propositions about it, but you have more episodes. Which of us then understands better? A consequence of this argument is the assertion that a valid measure of understanding of a concept involves eliciting the full set of elements the person has in memory about it. Also, assessment of the elicited set is subjective, as it depends on the weights the assessor gives to particular elements. Because I can define democracy, one judge may rate my understanding higher than yours; but because you have *lived* democracy and have episodes about it, another judge may prefer your understanding. These points will recur in later chapters when we look at each technique for probing understanding.

## Understanding of Whole Disciplines

The points that have been made about understanding of concepts apply with even greater force to the understanding of whole disciplines. The answer to the question, 'Did Einstein understand physics?' can only be 'to a degree'. The question 'Did Einstein understand physics better than Newton did?' might be answered 'yes', because we could judge that Einstein had all the relevant propositions and skills that Newton did, plus a good number more gained from his own work and the discoveries others made in the intervening centuries. Einstein's and Newton's images and episodes would have differed, but we might accept that this would not constitute a vital difference in their understandings. The question 'Did Einstein understand physics better than Bohr?' is much less easy to answer. We might value differently the contributions of each to knowledge, but it is hard to say whether the things Einstein believed about physics which his contemporary, Bohr, did not are more central to understanding of the subject than those that Bohr did not share with Einstein.

This argument implies that there is no central core of knowledge which is essential to the understanding of a discipline. That is not to say that all knowledge is of equal value or relevance in understanding. The judgement of that relevance must, however, be subjective. We are prepared to say that the proposition 'Shakespeare presented a Tudor version of the Wars of the Roses' is more central to the understanding of his plays than 'Boys played the parts of women in Shakespeare's time', or that 'A force is a push or a pull' is more central to the understanding of force than 'There are four fundamental sorts of force in the universe', but others may not agree.

Further subjectivity comes when we consider the person who is doing the understanding. We are more tolerant of the amount of knowledge that children should have before we say that they understand than we are for adults, especially adults who have a responsibility to know. We might say 'The Prime Minister does not understand the relation between President and Congress' and 'John Doe (year-10-student) understands the relation between President and Congress' while accepting that the Prime Minister does know much more about it than John Doe does. We just require more of Prime Ministers. Such is their lot.

In sum, understanding of a concept or of a discipline is a continuous function of the person's knowledge, is not a dichotomy and is not linear in extent. To say whether someone understands is a subjective judgement which varies with the judge and with the status of the person who is being judged. Knowledge varies in its relevance to understanding, but this relevance is also a subjective judgement.

## Understanding of Single Elements of Knowledge

Some different points arise when we consider the understanding of a single element, such as 'Longfellow wrote epic poems'. This proposition contributes to the understanding of the concepts of Longfellow and epic poems, but cannot be understood unless its believers or recipients have sufficient other elements associated with the labels 'Longfellow', 'wrote', 'epic', and 'poems' for each of these components to be understood to a reasonable degree. Skills of grammatical usage come into it too, since Longfellow has to be recognized as the name of a person even if nothing else is known about him. Just as it was not possible to specify the essential elements for understanding of a concept or discipline, so it is not possible to say which elements must be part of the constituent concepts in a proposition for it to be understood. It is again subjective.

Understanding of another of the six forms of element, intellectual skills, requires something more. Gagné (1965) defined several types of intellectual skills, of which one of the most important is algorithmic or rule-following knowledge. Rules can be learned as a procedure to be followed without understanding, as is often demonstrated in mathematics classes. The procedure is less rote, more meaningful, when labels are known for the concepts and operations in it and those labels are connected to many elements. For example, the complex skill of finding velocity at a point on a position–time graph involves the concepts velocity, displacement, time interval, slope or gradient, and tangent. The rule can be performed without knowing what these words mean, almost without seeing or hearing them, but is more comprehensible when they are understood. More central to understanding of a rule, however, is being able to explain the procedure. 'Why do you draw a tangent to the point where the velocity is to be found?' 'Because the tangent is the line which has the slope of the curve at that point'. 'Why does that matter?' and so on. These explanations must themselves be understood as propositions. They cannot be rote strings, learned as catechisms.

Although explanations are key parts of understanding of intellectual skills, and of propositions and other single elements, the nature of explanation itself turns out to be curiously difficult to describe. We might say, 'to explain is to give reasons for', but then we have to describe what is involved in giving reasons. In some cases this might not be too difficult. In explaining why in solving simple algebraic equations the numbers are gathered on one side and the x's on the other, we can appeal to episodes involving balances or can say it is so we can divide by the number in front of the x in the next step in order to find out what one x is worth. Sometimes it is not so easy. Why does light pass through glass and not through brick? Naming is not explaining, so we cannot get away with saying, it is because glass is transparent. There are many possible examples like that one, where a satisfying answer is hard to find. Often explanation comes down to putting things in more familiar terms and not pushing them to fundamentals, even though the explanation is essentially circular. Why do things fall? Because of gravity. But what then is gravity? That which makes things fall.

The explanations that most of us find best are those based on simple logic or on direct experience. An example of the first is why $x^o = 1$:

$$x^m \div x^n = x^{m-n}$$

$$\Rightarrow x^p \div x^p = x^{p-p} = x^o$$

But any number divided by itself equals 1

$$\Rightarrow x^o = 1.$$

An example of the second is why aeroplanes stay in the air. Although an explanation could be framed around Bernoulli's law of stream flow, that is less convincing to most people than demonstrating lift by blowing on the edge of a light piece of shaped wood or a sheet of paper. When direct experience is not possible, we are satisfied with analogies between the phenomenon and something we have experienced. Thus when we try to understand why Hitler invaded Russia, though we ourselves have not commanded armies or been dictator of a country, we make parallels with our own desires and frustrations that were felt in much smaller contexts.

## Understanding of Extensive Communications

When we talk of understanding of a proposition or a concept or a whole discipline, we are referring to a state of knowledge, the pattern of information that is linked to, or that constitutes, the target. It is a bit different for an extensive communication such as a poem, a speech, a painting, a play, a ballet, or a block of text. When we talk of understanding these sorts of things, we refer to a process rather than a state, the analysis of the words or other symbols to make a meaning.

Understanding of an extensive communication can be on two

levels. First there is the meaning of each of its constituent parts, and then there is the meaning of the whole, which may not be expressed so directly and may have to be inferred.

It is unlikely that the total meaning can be grasped without a reasonably detailed understanding of its constituent parts. A text cannot be comprehended unless the great majority of its sentences can be converted to propositions that are familiar, or that can be related immediately to elements that are present in memory. The relation need not be direct or complete, so long as some satisfactory identification is possible, as Lewis Carroll's poem about the Jabberwock will show:

> And as in uffish thought he stood,
> The Jabberwock, with eyes of flame,
> Came whiffling through the tulgey wood,
> And burbled as it came!

The words *uffish*, *whiffling*, and *tulgey* need not have been seen before for a reader to be able to form some understanding of the verse.

The Jabberwock example illustrates the importance of images in understanding. Humans thought in images long before they invented words, and we still feel more satisfied when we can translate words into images. Indeed, the essence of poetry is the use of words to evoke images, which in their turn are often linked to emotions. Imagery is also used in science, where complex notions are often represented by familiar, everyday images. Thus light is represented as a stream of solid particles, or as waves. Neither representation is exact, but we feel that we understand better the nature of light when we relate it to these familiar images. A useful approach to probing understanding may therefore be to elicit the person's images.

Communications need not be verbal. Ballet, mime, and painting are arts of non-verbal communication, while plays are both verbal and non-verbal (that is why it is possible to make some sense of a play or an opera which is presented in a language that you do not know). These non-verbal examples reveal that understanding of a communication is more than decoding the separate elements and checking that each is understood. The communication as a whole has to be considered. What is its theme, its main message? Is it a direct statement or an allegory? Is it transmission of new information or elaboration of old? What purpose lies behind its construction? Answers to such questions demonstrate the understanding. A child may read *Gulliver's Travels* as an adventure story, and understand it in terms of images of ships, giants, and so forth; but a more sophisticated reader derives a deeper understanding by appreciating it as a satire on the society of eighteenth century Britain.

Just as it takes time to read a book, so can it take time to comprehend a non-verbal communication that, on the surface, can be taken in more quickly. We might have to look long, and reflect intensely on, a great painting before we extract much of its meaning. What we extract is as much our construction as the painter's, so that young children can do little more than recognise the elements ('there's a house and a horse and a man with a dog, and there's a bird ...') where the adult can see a representation of a human dilemma or deep emotional experience. It is the adult's episodes and knowledge of history or society that make possible this deeper understanding. Therefore one approach to probing understanding of a communication would be to ask what experiences it made the respondent recall. The main implication of the discussion in this section, though, is that no measure of understanding of an extensive communication will be complete that does not include a call for a statement of the main theme.

## Understanding of Situations

People are always in one situation or another, usually commonplace ones with which they are entirely familiar, but occasionally novel ones which take a bit of effort to comprehend. In a way situations are like extensive communications in which the information is presented instantaneously rather than sequentially. This is not to mean that they cannot be dynamic, a succession of scenes unfolding one after another. Whether a single scene or a succession, understanding a situation involves seeing parallels between it and earlier experiences; that is, in Schank and Abelson's (1977) terms, having a script for it. Often this means being able to label the situation. Suppose, for instance, you are driving along a freeway when the traffic banks up and eventually stops. You understand this situation because you have been in something like it before and you can label it as a traffic jam.

In making sense of the situation, you do several things more or less unconsciously. You select and discard stimuli for attention, depending on how relevant you think they are to the situation. While in the traffic jam you may not take much note of the colours of the cars or the nature of the plants along the side of the freeway, but you do note the mass of cars in front of you and every nuance of their movement. Also, you are likely to think of explanations for how the situation arose: a crash, broken-down car, road repairs, and so on. And you will make predictions to yourself as to how the situation will develop: eventually the cars in front will move, the pace will be slow at first and there may be further stops, but eventually the traffic will move freely; and somewhere you will come to the cause of the delay, marked by a tow-truck or a repair gang or something.

The processes of selection, explanation, and prediction that are involved in making sense of situations can be focussed on in probes. To test your comprehension of the traffic jam we could ask you what is important here: the number of lanes, the makes of the cars, the time of day; and we would ask you why they are important. Or we could ask you to explain how this situation might have arisen, or to predict what will happen next. Of these three probes, that focus on selection, explanation, and prediction, only the third appears to have had much use in recent research, while none has had widespread use in schools or college practice. Examples in the techniques chapters are intended to remedy that, of course.

## Understanding of People

Understanding a person is very like understanding a situation. We have to feel able to explain why the person behaves as he or she does, and have to feel confident that we can predict at least the range of things the person might do. This book does not extend to probes of understanding of people, but it is clear how the notions of explanation and prediction might be used. We could ask respondents to explain why the target person behaves in such a way, and either judge the adequacy of the explanations ourselves or ask the target person to rate them. Also we could ask respondents to predict actions that the target person will undertake in certain situations, and then have them observe the actions and comment on any discrepancies between action and prediction.

## Construction of Meaning

We have described understanding as a function of the number of elements of knowledge the person possesses about the target, whether that target is a concept, a whole discipline, a situation, and so on, and of the mixture of different types of element and of the pattern of associations that the person perceives among them. This description is consistent with, and indeed owes much to, cognitive and constructivist theories of learning such as have been described by Piaget in numerous writings, Ausubel (1963, 1968), Wittrock (1974), and White (1988). The details of these theories differ, but an essential core to them is that learners construct their own meanings for the knowledge they acquire.

The person's understanding develops as new elements are acquired and linked with the existing pattern of associations between elements of knowledge. Addition of new elements will often stimulate reorganization of the pattern as the person reflects on the new knowledge and sees how it puts the older knowledge in a different light.

We can identify three ways in which construction of meaning occurs. One is where there is no immediate stimulus from outside the person, but through reflecting on knowledge the person perceives new links or deduces new propositions or creates new images. Sometimes this is accompanied by a sense of surprise — the 'ah-ha!' experience. An example happened to one of us recently, when he suddenly realised that Cap Finisterre translated to 'Land's End'; previously the name had meant nothing to him. A second form of construction of meaning occurs through incidental learning, when the person forms a new episode from a situation that was not deliberately designed to promote learning, and sees that that episode illuminates some knowledge. For example, one of us was walking through a forest when snow was on the ground, and noticed that leaves that had fallen had sunk deeply into the snow; suddenly he realised that this was a consequence of the principle that dark surfaces (the leaf) absorb heat better than light (the snow), and ever since that episode has added to his understanding of the principle. The third form is where meanings are constructed under the guidance of a teacher.

In all three forms the new understanding will be unique to the individual. It is obvious that that is so for the first two cases, but it is less widely appreciated that it holds for the third, too. Of course one would expect that where instruction is given to a whole class of students together that there will be similarities in the structures of knowledge formed in the students' minds. However, each of those minds is a different receptor — the patterns of episodes, images, and other elements will differ even if the students have been together in the same class for a long time. Hence, what they make of the instruction will differ and their understandings will not be the same. According to the arguments we made earlier, these differences cannot be represented by placements on a linear scale. Understanding is multi-dimensional.

### Assessment and Scoring

Our description of understanding has two key implications for its assessment: understanding is too complex to be assessed adequately by any single style of test; and a single numerical score, such as is commonly used following school tests, cannot represent satisfactorily a person's understanding. The first point is the spur to the production of this book; we advocate informed use of many different probes. The second point is associated with further implications that follow from the purposes of assessment.

A broad distinction can be made between assessment during a course of instruction for diagnosis intended to assist learning, and assessment at the end of the course that is intended to summarise the quality of the students' learning and to be used in decisions about the award of a qualification or entry to a further course. The first is termed formative, the second summative, assessment. As with many apparent dichotomies, the distinction between the two purposes is not absolute. Diagnostic tests are also used for summative purposes, and end-of-course tests can be used to aid subsequent learning.

The techniques described in the chapters that follow can be used for either purpose. They are excellent, specialised diagnostic tools. They can be part of summative tests, where they will not only reveal much about the quality of the students' learning that traditional tests would miss, but also will come to affect the strategies of learning that students apply. The presently limited styles of test in common use promote limited learning strategies, which result in limited under-standing. When students know that diverse and powerful probes are part of the summative tests, they will develop better learning strategies.

Although we have argued that understanding cannot be summed well by a single score, the prevailing acceptance of single scores from summative tests means that we have to give some attention in the description of each probe to how its outcomes can be scored. It will probably be apparent in each chapter that we do this grudgingly. We see understanding as too complex and fascinating a construct to be reduced to a number, but we are prepared to consider procedures for scoring if that will help attain our goal of achieving the widespread use of the powerful techniques that follow.

Chapter 2

# Concept Mapping

A concept map aims to show how someone sees the relations between things, ideas, or people. Most often, maps are used with the terms that make up the content of a series of lessons.

Figure 2.1 shows a concept map produced by an 11-year-old in a social studies class. The class had previously done a number of concept maps.

## Purposes of Concept Maps

How can you find out how students link ideas, or how they see the structure of a large topic? They may know individual facts, but how do they fit them together? The traditional approach to these problems has been to have students write essays. However, essays take students a long time to create, and almost as long for the teacher to read and evaluate. And even with all this effort, essays often do not give good information about how students see structure or link ideas. Other abilities, such as general vocabulary, writing style and the capacity to express ideas intrude on the reader's judgements and mask structuring and linking. Concept maps focus more specifically on the structure and linking that the student perceives. Once students understand the process of the task, concept maps are quicker (both for students to do and the teacher to consider), more direct and considerably less verbal than essays. Although for reasons that we set out later they should not be used too frequently, concept maps can be an important alternative to essays. Whether the concepts that make up a topic are abstractions, such as literary terms, or specific things or people, such as characters in a novel, mapping is a means of eliciting the relations each student perceives between the concepts.

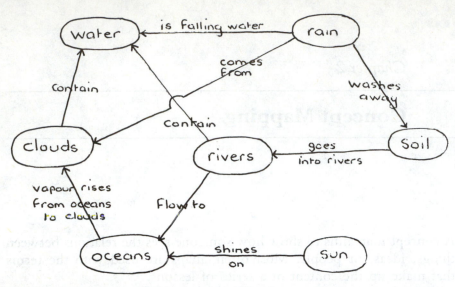

*Figure 2.1: An example of a concept map*

## Procedure

There are several discrete steps that students should go through in producing a concept map. On the first occasion that concept maps are given to a group there are special points that are described in the section 'Introducing Concept Maps to Students'; the present section covers the basic procedure for students who have done maps before.

To illustrate the procedure that we recommend for generating concept maps we will use the concepts *animals, plants, living things, cow, dog, grass.*

### Materials

While students are thinking about their concept map, it is important for them to be able to manipulate physically the concept labels. Hence each student is given a set of cards, about 3 cm × 1 cm. On each card is the name of one of the concepts or ideas to be mapped. The number of cards in the set will vary according to the type of concept, the purpose the teacher has for the map, and the sophistication of the students, but will usually be from about six to twenty. Each student

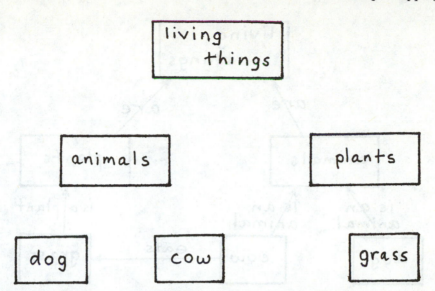

*Figure 2.2:   A concept map at the stage of arranging the terms on the sheet*

also has a sheet of paper on which to arrange the cards, and some means, such as sticky tape or glue, of fixing the cards to the paper when the arrangement is complete. The sheet of paper should be large enough to permit plenty of space between the cards.

*Instructions*

The teacher gives the following instructions, one step at a time. These can be oral, or (better) displayed on a board or screen.

1   Sort through the cards, and put to one side any that have a term you don't know or which you think is not related to any other term.
2   Put the remaining cards on the sheet of paper, and arrange them in a way that makes sense to you. Terms you see as related should be kept fairly close together, but leave space between even the closest cards.
3   When you are satisfied with your arrangement of the cards, stick them to the sheet. (So, for our example, a student might at this stage have a sheet like that in Figure 2.2.)
4   Draw lines between the terms you see to be related.

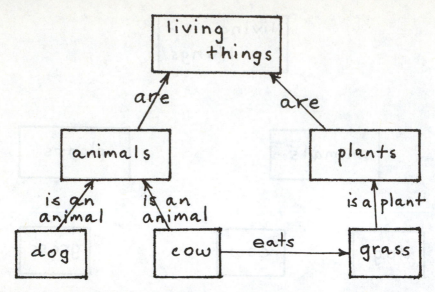

*Figure 2.3:    The completed map*

5   Write on each line the nature of the relation between the terms. It can help to put an arrowhead on the line to show how to read the relation. (So our student might now have a sheet like Figure 2.3.)
6   If you put any cards to one side in the first step, go back to these and see if you now want to add any to the map. If you do add any make sure you write the nature of the links between them and the other terms.

*Comments on These Instructions*

1   Step 5 (students writing the nature of the links they see) is *crucial*. Without this the concept mapping technique is of little value. In our experience students often find writing the relations the most irksome part of the procedure, and would skip it if they could.
2   Some concept maps are hierarchical, that is the relations between the terms are inclusive with general terms standing above more specific ones. The *living things* example is an instance. For these hierarchical maps it is worth suggesting in step 2 that students begin by selecting the concept that includes all or most of the others, then the next most inclusive and so on. However, since

many maps are not hierarchical (e.g., Figures 2.4 and 2.8), this modification of step 2 should be used discriminatingly.

3 We have phrased the instructions in language appropriate for middle secondary school students. For young primary school or tertiary (college) students, changes in language might be desirable.

4 Obviously, as students become familiar with the process of producing concept maps the instructions become more of the form of reminders.

5 The teacher should do the concept map before giving the task to the students. It is only when you attempt the map yourself that you see which concepts should be included and which might be left out from the set given to the students. The teacher's map will be useful later, too, when the students' maps are discussed.

## Examples of Concept Maps

We have chosen examples to illustrate the range of areas in which concept mapping can be used, points that need to be considered in using maps, and the range of student responses that might be expected.

Figure 2.4 shows two maps, by 14-year-old students who had just finished reading the novel *Z for Zachariah*. Note that the terms included characters, objects, events, and emotions. There are substantial differences between the two maps. Student 2 has produced a map which is quite linear, with no links apart from the linear chain. On the other hand, student 1 has many cross linkages and gives evidence of a much more integrated structure.

The two maps in Figure 2.5 show different qualities of response to a hierarchical pattern of relations. We rearranged the second map slightly (without changing any of the links) so that it is easier to see that it contains all of the links in the first map plus many others. It was particularly interesting to see that the second student put in links that were not part of the unit as the teacher taught it. Maps allow students to display knowledge they have acquired elsewhere.

The maps of Figure 2.6 were done by physics graduates in a pre-service teacher education course. They differ markedly in quality, particularly in regard to the amount of cross-linking. The first map is almost totally linear, while the second is much more integrated. In the second map, the student has felt the need to add a concept (density), a most appropriate action. Even though the second map is much more impressive, it also shows a common difficulty with one pair of

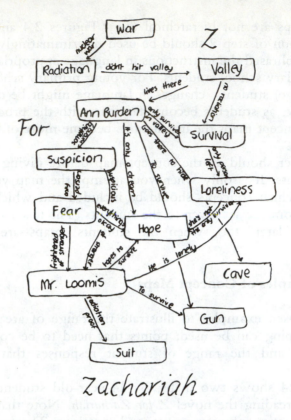

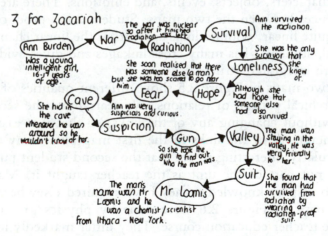

*Figure 2.4:* Concept maps for terms from a novel (from Baird and Mitchell, 1986, pp. 118–19)

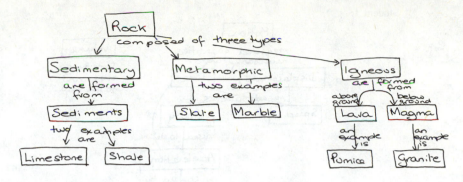

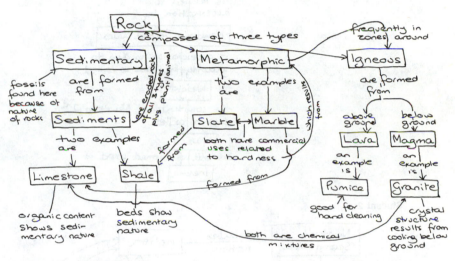

*Figure 2.5: Hierarchical maps produced by two 15-year-olds*

concepts that can cause substantial problems in learning those ideas. That is the view that inertia is 'resistance to force' rather than the property which determines how a given force will affect the motion of the object.

Another point that these examples raise is the speed with which older students learn to produce revealing concept maps. This was the first serious map done by these students. Younger students sometimes need a little more practice, but not always.

The example in Figure 2.7 is by a 9-year-old, and shows that even quite young children can learn to make sensible and informative concept maps.

**Student 1:**

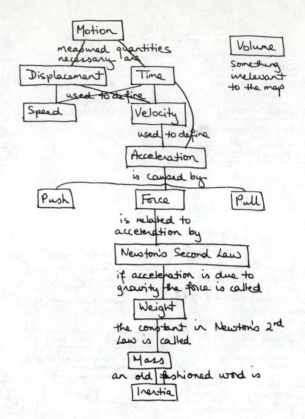

**Student 2:**

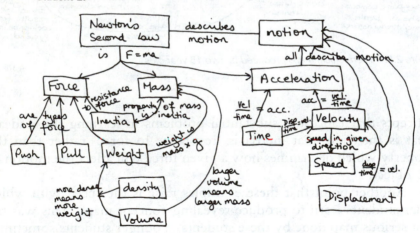

*Figure 2.6: Maps illustrating different extents of cross-linking*

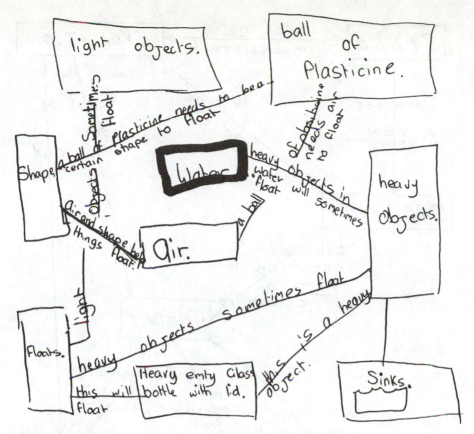

*Figure 2.7: A concept map produced by a younger student*

We include the map of Figure 2.8 to show how a map with a small number of terms can reveal quickly a complex structure of ideas about sophisticated concepts. It also allows us to make the point that maps can be supplemented with interviews. In discussion following completion of the map, the interviewer elicited the constructor's opinions that evolution is not a view of creation since it does not postulate how life began; and that the word 'theory' is sometimes used colloquially to mean a guess, which is not the meaning he had for it here and explains why he put in the link 'theory is *not* some form of poor quality fact'.

The example also shows that when there are only a few terms being mapped it can be revealing to ask for multiple links between concepts.

The three maps in Figure 2.9 were made by 15-year-old students. Their teacher wanted to explore how well they distinguished between

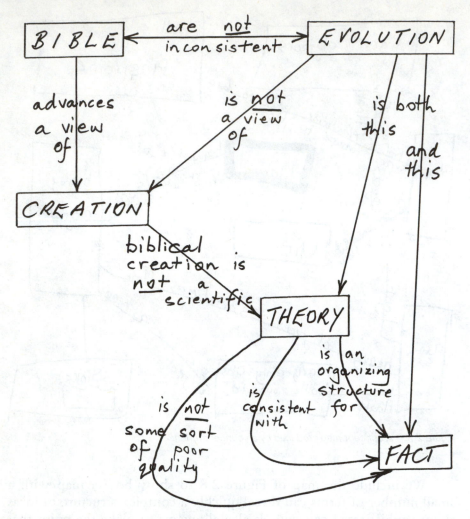

*Figure 2.8: A complex structure of beliefs revealed by a small number of terms*

static and current electricity. The first two were among the poorer ones produced in the class.

Map 1 reveals a low level of understanding. It has few links, with a star formation in which only the central concept is linked to more than one other concept. The connection between *electrons* and *static* is either vague or shows an erroneous conception.

Map 2 has more linkages, but represents another inadequate understanding. The leaving of three links unlabelled may indicate vagueness or may merely be an oversight; the teacher could clear that

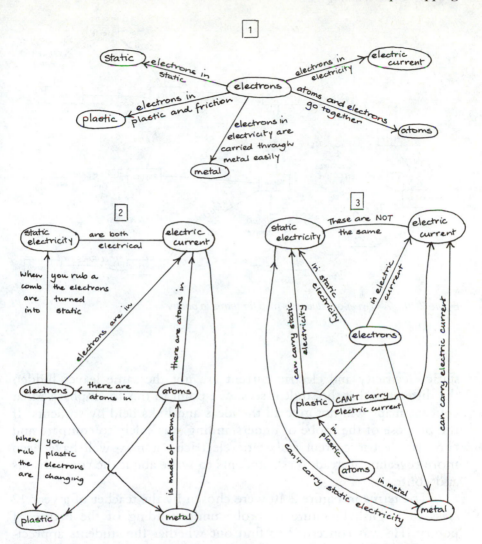

*Figure 2.9:   A variety of understandings revealed by maps*

up by asking the student. One might conject that the link 'there are atoms in electrons' is a misinterpretation of earlier teaching that 'everything is made of atoms'. Changing that notion is an essential first step in improving the student's understanding of the whole set of concepts. Thus the concept map revealed a key problem in the student's ideas.

Map 3 is better than the other two: there are plenty of links and all are labelled sensibly. However, the link at the top which states that

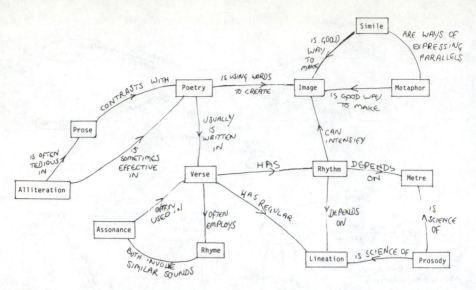

*Figure 2.10:    A 17-year-old student's map for terms in poetry*

static electricity and electric current are not the same leaves hidden the difference that the student sees. We point to this to emphasise that concept maps will not give all the ideas and links held by students. If the purpose of the probe of understanding was solely to compare and contrast electric current and static electricity it may well have been more revealing instead to ask students to write about the comparisons and contrasts.

The terms in Figure 2.10 were chosen by the teacher of a year 12 class in English literature to probe understanding of the nature of poetry. He was concerned to find out whether the students appreciated his belief that poetry is synonymous with imagery. It would be hard to devise a valid test of that. If you simply asked the students 'What is the relation between poetry and imagery?' they might parrot off the statement that they are synonymous but might not have processed the statement deeply, nor have expressed it spontaneously. The concept map allows a light touch in probing this knowledge.

The map in Figure 2.11 illustrates two points. Firstly, if you ask students to place arrowheads on links, they will not always be consistent in the way they use them. Secondly, the probable strength of an idea, in this example that *island* is a defining characteristic of *country* and *continent*, may be indicated by its presence in a number of links. Presumably this idea, which may be common among Australian stu-

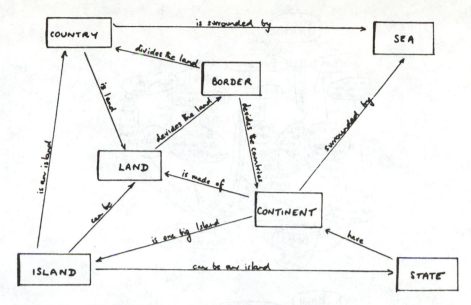

*Figure 2.11: Arrowheads in maps (from Baird and Mitchell, 1986)*

dents, must be challenged by the teacher before a better understanding of the concepts can be achieved.

Concept maps can be used in subjects that are rarely tested on paper. Figure 2.12 shows two maps on basketball done by a player early and late in a season. The player chose his own terms. He was influenced by a map prepared by his coach to guide the players in training. The coach's map is shown in Novak and Gowin (1984, pp. 50–1).

While it is true that a knowledge of the content area on which a concept map focuses is necessary for interpreting the map, we suspect that even those readers with no knowledge of basketball will see the increased complexity and integration, and greater structural organization, in the second map. Novak and Gowin report that the performance of this player improved greatly through the period between the two maps, though we do not mean to imply that doing the maps was a major influence on that.

## Introducing Concept Maps to Students

As with any new task, students take time to learn how to make concept maps. By way of analogy, imagine you were teaching a

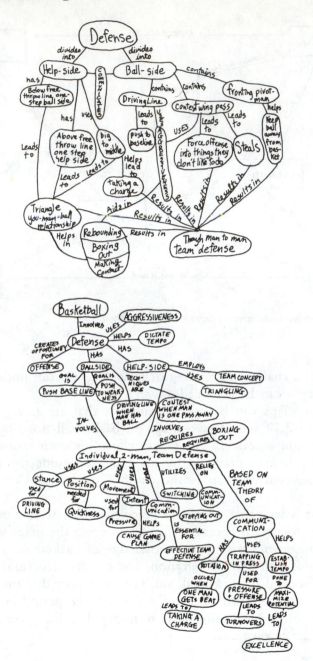

*Figure 2.12:* Basketball maps made by a player early and late in a season (from Novak and Gowin, *Learning to Learn*, Cambridge University Press, 1984, pp. 44–5)

group of students who had never seen a multiple choice test question. Before asking them such questions, you would want to give them some idea of how to go about answering them. The same applies to concept mapping: students need some understanding of how to do the task before their concept maps can be helpful to you (and them) as an assessment of their learning.

Recommendations follow for the first occasion on which students do a concept map.

1   Begin with a simple topic, familiar to students so that it is easier for them to concentrate on learning the process. Use a relatively small number of terms. A suitable well-known topic can often be from outside the subject you are teaching. For example, one set of concepts which could be used to introduce concept maps to 15-year-olds is the *living things* example given above. For 11-year-olds in a primary school a good set might be *food, meat, vegetables, mutton, beef, peas, carrots.*

2   It can be helpful to introduce concept maps by doing one in front of the class. By using an overhead projector and small pieces of acetate as the cards you can work through a concept map while allowing the whole class to see what you are doing and hear you working aloud. This can give students something to model when they attempt their first, simple map.

3   As they are doing their first map, emphasise to students the importance of thinking about all possible links and of writing down the nature of each link. Point out that not all terms are necessarily linked, and there are occasions when it is not clear whether or not a link exists. In this last case, negative links (i.e., A is not related to B) should be ignored.

4   Students are unlikely to produce good maps at their first attempt. If the first maps are poor, discuss the task and their maps and then give the students a second attempt at the same map, preferably with one or two extra related terms (e.g., for the *living things* maps above, you could add *trees* and *water*).

5   You might give a suggested layout for their first map, or one possible link. If you do, it is important to remove these prompts from subsequent maps.

6   Help students realise that there is no single, correct answer to the task. There is often more than one appropriate link between a pair of concepts, and layouts can vary considerably.

In our experience some groups accept this point immediately while for others it has to be reiterated.

**Variations and Extensions**

The variations that are listed below are intended to illustrate the range of possible procedures rather than be exhaustive. We have found that teachers like to change procedures to suit the subject and topic and the age and experience of their students. The purpose for the map also influences the choice, so we have grouped the variations accordingly.

*1 The Purpose Is to Explore Understanding of a Limited Aspect of the Topic*

Choice of the terms to be mapped can direct the focus of the probe. For example, if you want to check whether the students understand practical application of theoretical principles, the list of terms can be slanted to include one or two instances or applications. For example, an appropriate list of terms for a concept map to be given to 15-year-olds who have been studying electricity might be *current, circuit, electric charge, electrical energy, resistance, potential difference, heat.* An extension to see how the students relate these concepts to electrical appliances can be achieved by adding *light globe* to the list of terms. The application term can be given after the original map is complete, or together with the conceptual terms. If the latter course is adopted, thought should be given to reducing the number of conceptual terms in order to focus on the applications. In the electrical example above, *electric charge* or *circuit* might be omitted.

Other examples include: in senior history, *coup d'etat, revolution, civil unrest, autocrat, dictator* with one or two of *Franco, Hitler, William III, Cromwell, Henry IV.* For the list of terms used with senior primary school students which is shown in Figure 2.1, add *plants.*

Another form of limitation is where, instead of seeing how students structure a dozen or more terms covering all of a topic, you want to probe more deeply the relations they see between two or three important terms. In that case limit the terms to those key ones and ask the students to make *multiple* links between them. Figure 2.13 is an example.

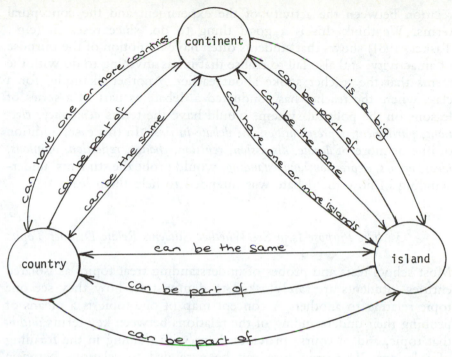

*Figure 2.13: Multiple links between a few terms*

## 2 The Purpose Is to Check Whether Students Understand the Reasons for a Lesson

Often a teacher may want to check whether the students understand why they are doing a particular activity, such as a classroom experiment. This can be at two levels: understanding of how the activity relates cognitively to the content being learned (i.e., do the students see what content the activity is designed to teach?); and understanding why this activity was used instead of some alternative (i.e., do students understand the way in which the activity might help them learn?). As an example of the first of these, consider primary school students learning about reflection of light who undertake an experiment using mirrors. A set of terms for a concept map might be *mirrors, light, objects, images, light source*. If, after the students have finished their maps, the teacher asks them to add *experiment with mirrors*, the way they do that will reveal their understanding of the

31

relation between the activity of the experiment and the conceptual terms. We think this is a good thing to do, since research (e.g., Tasker, 1981) shows that students often have no notion of the purpose of an activity, and also fail to realise that it has anything to do with the terms that the teacher spoke about earlier. Another example, for a class where the teacher has conducted a debate as part of a series of lessons on the political system, would have the terms *democracy, elections, parliament, representatives, the debate in class.* In this case, addition of one or more of *debate, discussion, revision, change, reflection, opinions, ideas, values, expression, understanding,* would probe the students' understanding of how the debate was intended to help them learn.

### 3  The Purpose Is to See Whether Students Relate Distinct Topics

Most school tests and probes of understanding treat topics as isolated entities. Students are rarely asked to demonstrate how they see one topic relating to another. A concept map of one topic is a means of probing their understanding of the relations between key terms *within* that topic, and of course provides them with training in the forming of relations. The procedure can be extended to relations between topics that otherwise might be seen as distinct and unconnected. The practical problem is that the number of terms in the two (or more) topics may be too great for the students to handle all at once. The solution is to keep the concept maps they do for each topic, then at the appropriate time return them with the instruction that they are to link the separate maps by lines between related terms, and are to write the form of the relations on the lines. Students who have learned the topics as isolated blocks of knowledge will find it difficult to produce many links. Again, this is a fine training procedure, awakening students to the possibility of, and need to look for, links between topics. It is particularly useful where they have done concept maps in different subjects. For instance, one on an aspect of nineteenth century political history can be linked with another on modes of transport and even another on scientific concepts and inventions.

### 4  The Purpose Is to Probe Appreciation of Which Concepts Are the Key Ones

Instead of giving the students cards bearing the names of the concepts, give them blank cards on which they have to place their own selections of key terms, or perhaps a mixture of cards with and without names. In either case it is wise to specify an upper limit to the number of cards to be used, and to describe the scope of the map by specifying a sequence of lessons or a section of textbook that it is to cover.

Teachers should give this extended task only to students who are experienced in the basic procedure. Also it must be appreciated that older students will, normally, be able to supply and cope with larger numbers of concepts. In half-year and year-long post-graduate and pre-service teacher training courses, students have produced well-constructed maps with over a hundred concepts.

Users of concept maps may see advantage in a combination of the free-range and controlled procedures, in which the students are first asked to provide their individual lists of key terms from which a single set is determined for all to use in making maps.

### 5 The Purpose Is to Identify Changes in Relations that Students Perceive between Concepts

As a rule, tests are used much less before a course of instruction than after, even though it is a well-established dictum that it helps in teaching to know what the learners understand about the topic to start with. Perhaps one reason why pre-tests are less popular is that students react badly to being asked about something that they have not been taught before, or at least recently. They sometimes have the same reaction to doing a concept map before a series of lessons, though mapping, being open and less concerned with right answers, is less threatening.

If students do accept the task of doing a map before the series of lessons, the teacher can compare that map with one done at the end and should learn much about the developments in their knowledge. An even more valuable use of the before and after maps is for the students to compare their own pair, analysing and writing about the changes. Their written comments provide further information about their understanding of the topic, and the task is a powerful learning experience.

Concept maps can be used to identify changes as they occur in the course of a sequence of instruction, as well as just between the beginning and the end. For example, Figure 2.14 contains two concept maps made by the same student at different times during a university course on genetics. Students had to generate their own terms for the first map, which they made after a lecture on polygenic

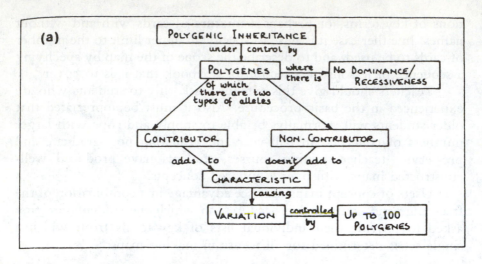

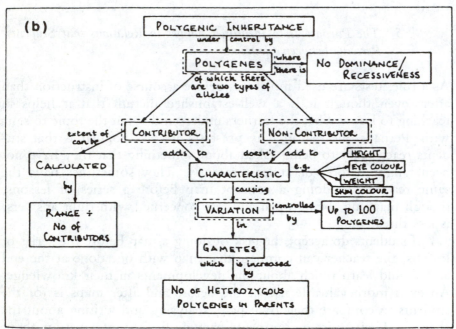

*Figure 2.14:   Changes in structure of knowledge during a course (from Kinnear, Gleeson and Comerford, 1985, p. 107)*

inheritance. They did the second map after a subsequent laboratory exercise. For the second map, the lecturer gave the students a copy of their first map and asked them to modify it by adding new terms, by making any corrections they felt necessary and to indicate in another colour any terms or links which they now felt they understood better.

## 6   The Purpose Is to Promote Discussion

Here we move away from the probing of individuals' understanding to the use of concept maps in promoting learning.

We have found that concept maps promote serious debate, even among students less likely to participate in the usual forms of class discussion. Perhaps this is because the task is purposeful and involves physical acts, or because there is no single correct answer. No-one's map is ever so bad as to be condemned out of hand (we have yet to find the concept map equivalent of 0 per cent on a mathematics exam). On the other hand, no single map is ever demonstrably better than all the rest. The contrast with traditional forms of tests of detail is marked. It is rare for students to perceive competitive threat in concept mapping, although the intellectual demand of the task cannot be denied. This friendly aspect of this form of probing of student understanding is why we prefer to use concept maps in teaching rather than in summative assessment.

Discussion of the relations between the terms in a topic is stimulated by having the students work in small groups, best from two to five people, to make a map. Although learning is the focus, the teacher can discover much about the students' understanding by listening to the points that they make. Students who are too shy to speak up in a large class often contribute freely in the co-operative and unthreatening activity of map-making.

The procedure can be extended by having the whole class compare and comment on the various groups' maps. Teachers do not do this often these days with individuals' work, since they are aware of the unfortunate emotional consequences for many children, whether praised or criticised. However, reactions to group work are less personal, and appear more beneficial. Again, the absence of 'rightness' and 'wrongness' with maps is an advantage. Students are happy to accept that other groups put in a link that they did not, and though they might defend their omission are likely to consider covertly the point and to learn from it. Teachers can encourage this by directing them to think about questions such as 'Would my map be better with the addition of that link? If so, why? If not, why not?', 'What aspects of the topic does the map suggest I do not understand well? What should I do about this?'

Our experience is that students at all levels much prefer doing concept maps in groups, to the extent that once they have done one as a group it can sometimes be difficult to get them to do them as individuals in class. The solution is to set an individual map as a homework exercise.

## What the Procedure Reveals

It should be apparent from the examples that have been given that concept maps show how students see the structure of a topic, in contrast with the detail that short-answer tests or even extended essays reveal. They are a means for seeing the shape of the wood, not the state of individual trees. And so they complement rather than replace the tests of detail.

The way in which students conceive the structure of a topic tells much about the quality of their learning. A poor concept map coupled with reasonable performance on a test of detail suggests that this student's learning may be rote, and hence that the knowledge will soon be lost. The student may need training in a more effective learning style, being encouraged to reflect on the relations between one concept and another rather than focussing exclusively on detail. A rich and justifiable map that is sharply different from the teacher's notion of the topic reveals an original mind. But if the map is not sensible then a number of possibilities exist: erroneous links between concepts (such as the atoms-electrons link in the second map in Figure 2.9) indicate a specific shortcoming in understanding; an unreasonable or inexplicable structure may suggest an undisciplined mind. A poor, unstructured map coupled with poor performance on a test of detail can certainly be dispiriting for the student, but can also be helpful diagnostically. Does the student fail at detail because no structure is perceived? If so, the student might improve if the teacher makes the structure clear at the outset. Or does the student see no structure because no detail has been learned? If so, then different, and obvious, action is necessary.

As well as information about individuals, the maps reveal the understanding present in the whole class, and hence tell much about the effectiveness of the teaching. If many omit a relation that the teacher saw as crucial, such as the poetry–imagery one in Figure 2.10, then the teacher has failed and must reconsider how to develop an understanding of this point.

If the maps are alike, whether good or bad, the teaching had a powerful converging effect. Often that is the intent, but sometimes divergent maps may have been the goal if the topic had required creative effort in which students were to form their own patterns of links.

Of the six targets of understanding identified in Chapter 1, concept maps appear best suited to probing understanding of a whole discipline, or at least a substantial chunk of one. Of course the larger the topic the less sensitive the probe; what set of terms, for instance, would do to assess understanding of all history? The topic has to be kept within reasonable bounds, so that although all history may not be encompassed it might not be too difficult to put together a set for the French Revolution. If physics is too great, then maybe mechanics can be covered.

Since maps elicit the relations students see between the concepts that make up a topic, naturally they reveal something of the understanding that the students have of the individual concepts as well as of the whole topic. However, concept mapping is not an effective, nor efficient, method of probing understanding of a single concept. It does not reveal enough detail, yielding at best only a few propositions that involve the concept and no images, episodes, or other elements of knowledge.

A potential use of concept maps is to probe understanding of social situations or of a single person, where the terms may be names of people plus emotions, motives, or actions. This use would be similar to applying concept mapping to a novel, opera, or play. As far as we know, no-one has used the procedure with a real situation. The use with novels and so forth falls under the heading of assessing understanding of extensive communications. While there may be important aspects of the understanding that a concept map will miss, such as knowledge of the main themes, a map will reveal whether the patterns of relationships and actions are understood. This is illustrated in Figure 2.4. It would, then, be a useful complement to more precise probes of understanding of an extensive communication.

Understanding of the remaining type of target, single elements of knowledge, is not suitable for assessment by concept mapping.

### Scoring of Concept Maps

Whether or not to score concept maps is a question related to the teacher's purposes. If these are for formative assessment (that is, assessment aimed at promoting learning), then scoring probably is not helpful. Scoring becomes more sensible when concept maps are used in summative assessment (that is, assessment aimed at measuring learning outcomes on completion of a course or topic), though even then many teachers may feel, as we do, that giving any form of grade to a map can alter students' attitudes to them and so threaten their potential to promote learning.

Several writers describe methods of scoring concept maps. Novak and Gowin (1984), for example, suggest scoring on a number of criteria: the number and meaningfulness of links between concepts; the extent to which the map shows appropriate hierarchy among the concepts; the existence of links between different parts of the concept hierarchy; the provision of appropriate examples. These criteria apply only to hierarchical concept maps. We have indicated already that only some concept mapping tasks are hierarchical, and so the procedures should be used with discrimination if at all.

Although in reality maps do not divide neatly into hierarchical and non-hierarchical types, we consider them separately here. For those concept maps which are hierarchical (e.g., Figures 2.3 and 2.5) it is much more possible that there is something like a correct answer. If we compare their scoring with the scoring of essays, we see this type of concept map as akin to content-focussed essays on 'The Rift Valley of Africa', or 'Kerensky and the Russian Revolution', or 'The role of Sir Henry Parkes in the Federation of Australia', or 'The physics of motor car safety'. That is, there is parallel with essays in which the inclusion of particular content is expected. For such essays, scoring is often based on the presence of key facts and on the way these facts are placed in context. Marks are lost when important facts are omitted. Much the same approach can be applied to a hierarchical map, in which some subordinate relations simply must be present. As with content-based essays, the weighting to be given to the criteria, for the number and appropriateness of links and the presence of cross links, reflects the purposes and values of the teacher.

Non-hierarchical maps are often more revealing because of the greater diversity of patterns they admit. This diversity makes them more difficult to score. Scoring them has parallels with scoring essays that are meant to display writing style or ability to construct an argument or to present a coherent point of view rather than knowledge of content.

Methods for scoring non-hierarchical maps depend on teachers having first constructed their own maps, which, as we have said, is sensible practice anyway. The methods include the highly subjective one of gaining a general impression from inspecting the map, comparing it with the teacher's, and giving a global score in the same manner as marks are often determined for creative writing; and another of giving credit for the number of links that are the same as those on the teacher's map, with variations such as subtractions for incorrect links or additions for particularly insightful links.

Our suggestions for scoring may strike people as being vague. That is deliberate. In part it is because of our personal preference not to score concept maps, and in part because the method of scoring will depend on the purpose for which the scores are wanted. Whatever the purpose, we would expect that teachers (and students) would accept as good maps those that display considerable detail, variety of types of relation, rich patterns of cross-relations rather than simple chains, and clear structure; and as poor maps those with blocks of terms lumped together without clear relations, simple chains, and lines without statements.

## Using Concept Maps in Teaching

A principle that recurs throughout this book is that good testing devices are good teaching devices. Concept maps are indeed useful in promoting learning. We have already described how the construction of a map by a group encourages discussion and reflection, but even individual mapping helps learning. When individual maps are done in class, the teacher can move about, observing, questioning, and discussing, as well as encouraging students to write on each line. Many opportunities will occur for helpful teaching, opportunities that are rarer or harder to grasp in the usual teacher-centred style of lesson.

As they complete their maps students can compare them and discuss similarities and differences. The teacher can encourage and guide these discussions. Whole-class discussion led by the teacher is a further chance for productive teaching. In it the teacher may want to point out key relations that he or she had attempted to make clear and had hoped to see on everyone's map. For instance, in the poetry map of Figure 2.10, the teacher had intended that all the students would

appreciate that poetry and imagery are closely related, indeed synonymous; the post-mapping discussion would focus on the students'
representations of the relation between these two terms.

Of course, both the observations made during the mapping and
the quality of the whole-class discussion provide further information
about the students' understanding of the topic. The value of concept
mapping as a probe lies not only in the product, that is the maps
themselves, but in the process that can be observed while they are
being constructed. Reflection on what the maps reveal about teaching
can cause reconsideration of teaching style, for instance of the emphases put on different aspects of learning such as acquisition of facts
versus perceiving relations between topics, or of the balance between
getting students' knowledge to converge with that of the teacher and
encouraging them to develop their own views and be creative.

Teachers can devise variations in the mapping procedure to
promote particular sorts of learning as well as for different purposes in
assessment. You might, for instance, develop students' understanding
of similarities and differences between related terms by having them
replace one term on a completed map with another, and considering
the adjustments which the map then needs. For example, on the
photosynthesis map in Figure 2.15, replace photosynthesis with res-
piration.

You can use concept maps to help students link a new concept
into their ideas. After producing a relevant map using known concepts, introduce and discuss the new concept and then consider how it
can be added to their maps.

You can use concept maps to promote linking in new ways and
to stimulate higher order thinking. By selecting widely separated (but
connected) terms, you can promote divergent thinking. This is particularly useful for bridging traditionally separate subjects such as politics and technology.

A further use of concept maps in teaching is in planning lessons.
It is helpful for the teacher to do a concept map in order to determine
the sequence of presentation of ideas and to identify relations that are
to be emphasised. The value of this was brought home to us by the
experience of a teacher we know. He intended to have his class do a
concept map at the end of lessons on photosynthesis, and, as is good
practice, first did the map himself to check that he had selected
appropriate terms. Figure 2.15 shows his map.

The teacher asserts that doing the map caused him to change his
approach to teaching the topic. He decided that he should emphasise
the dual change nature of photosynthesis — change of molecules and

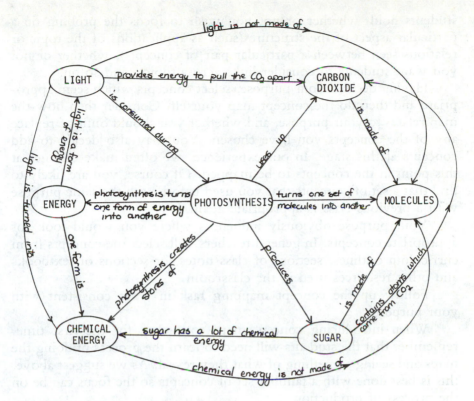

*Figure 2.15:   Trial map constructed by a teacher*

transformation of energy — which until then had not been apparent to him.

The teacher's experience demonstrates another instance of how important it is to write on each line the nature of the link. Diagrams superficially similar to concept maps are often used as flow charts in course outlines, but since they do not show explicitly the nature of the links between concepts cannot be helpful in the way the photosynthesis map was to our acquaintance.

## A Summary of Issues to Consider in Generating Concept Mapping Tasks

From the many purposes we suggest for concept maps in this chapter, select the purpose you have for the task. Whether the task is for formative or summative assessment will be obvious. Thereafter, consider whether you want to probe the general structure of a topic that students hold, whether or not you wish to focus the probing on a particular aspect of the structure (such as applications of the topic or relations seen between a particular pair of concepts), whether or not you want students to consider links across topics, and so on.

Having decided your purpose, select concepts which seem appropriate and then do the concept map yourself. Consider then how the map relates to your purpose, and whether you should omit or replace any of the concepts you have chosen. You may also decide to add concepts at this stage. In our experience, we often make changes at this point in the concepts to be mapped. Of course, you are likely to find that a set of concepts that you used before with the same purpose with a previous class is appropriate again.

Your purpose obviously influences where you would look for appropriate concepts. In general teachers will select the concepts from curriculum outlines, sections of class notes, or sections of textbooks and other resources used in the classroom.

Follow up the concept mapping task in ways consistent with your purpose.

When introducing concept maps to a class for the first time, remember that the students will need to learn the process of doing the maps and seeing something of what they reveal. As we suggest above, this is best done with a familiar set of concepts so the focus can be on the process of production.

We end with a caution. Although students usually like concept maps, they can be overdone. Constructing concept maps involves intellectual effort, and if they are required too frequently students will stop putting in that effort and will produce superficial, useless maps. Therefore avoid over-using them, or consistently using them for only one of the many purposes described in this chapter.


## Further Reading

BAIRD, J.R. and MITCHELL, I.J. (1986) *Improving the Quality of Teaching and Learning: An Australian Case Study — The Peel Project,* Melbourne: Monash University Printery. Accounts by teachers of their attempts to generate metacognitive behaviour in secondary school students. Some examples of concept maps are given.

FISHER, K.M., FALETTI, J., PATTERSON, H., THORNTON, R., LIPSON, J. and SPRING, C. (1990) 'Computer-based concept mapping: SemNet Software, a tool for describing knowledge networks', *Journal of College Science Teaching,* **19**, pp. 347–52. Describes a means of building up large concept maps on personal computers.

GUNSTONE, R.F., MITCHELL, I.J. and the MONASH CHILDREN'S SCIENCE GROUP (1988) 'Two teaching strategies for considering children's science', in *The Yearbook of the International Council of Associations for Science Education*, pp. 1–12. Describes concept maps and how to use them in teaching, in the context of secondary science teaching.

NOVAK, J.D. and GOWIN, D.B. (1984) *Learning How to Learn*, Cambridge: Cambridge University Press. Gives a detailed discussion of concept maps, their purposes, and their scoring. Focuses on concept maps with a hierarchical structure.

*Chapter 3*

# Prediction — Observation — Explanation

Prediction — Observation — Explanation, which we abbreviate to POE, probes understanding by requiring students to carry out three tasks. First they must predict the outcome of some event, and must justify their prediction; then they describe what they see happen; and finally they must reconcile any conflict between prediction and observation.

Figure 3.1 shows a student's response to a POE task which was given in the first week of a university physics course. The two balls used for the tasks were a shot put and a solid rubber ball of the same volume, with the shot put having a weight about 30 times that of the rubber ball.

The example in Figure 3.1 is of an event that students could see. The POE procedure can also be adapted to events that cannot be observed directly, so that it can be applied in history, literature and mathematics as well as in science and physical education. The section on 'Variations and Extensions' describes this adaptation, but first we shall establish the nature and purpose of POE tasks through examples that allow direct observation.

### Purposes of POE Tasks

An important purpose of education is for students to learn how to use the information they acquire to interpret events and experiences. Questions in lessons and in examinations commonly call for application of knowledge, often by asking for examples of a concept or a

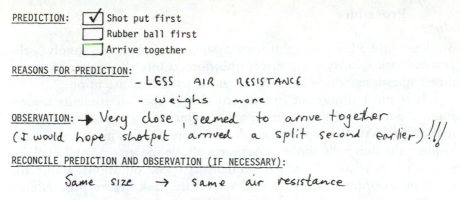

PREDICTION:  ☑ Shot put first
            ☐ Rubber ball first
            ☐ Arrive together

REASONS FOR PREDICTION:
            - LESS AIR RESISTANCE
            - weighs more

OBSERVATION: → Very close, seemed to arrive together
(I would hope shotput arrived a split second earlier) !//

RECONCILE PREDICTION AND OBSERVATION (IF NECESSARY):
            Same size → same air resistance

*Figure 3.1:   Response to a POE task involving two balls dropped together from a height of about 2 metres*

phenomenon or a situation, or for explanations. The POE task is another measure of ability to apply knowledge.

POE is often more direct than the usual style of question in revealing understanding. Its directness comes from its focus on a specific event. Consider again the example of Figure 3.1. A more common way of using this situation to assess ability to apply knowledge would be to ask a single question of the form 'Explain why, when we drop two balls of different weight from a height of about two metres, they appear to arrive at the ground at the same time'. When asked in this way, with the outcome of the event given in the question, students merely have to explain a completely described phenomenon. Often this will involve a rather unthinking reproduction of textbook knowledge. On the other hand, a prediction is more likely to require genuine application of the knowledge that the respondent believes to be most pertinent. Since the event is not fully described — a prediction is required — it is more likely that the student will have to use knowledge to reason out an answer. Also the student is more likely to evaluate how physics knowledge applies to the real situation, where the actual balls are shown, than the more general 'two balls of different weights' of the alternative question.

A key characteristic of POE is that the student must decide what reasoning to apply. We have found students frequently support predictions for the falling balls by everyday experiences and beliefs, or by knowledge which is at odds with physics such as 'gravity pulls equally hard on all objects'. This illustrates the greater power of the POE task than more usual approaches to probe the nature of the beliefs which students use to interpret real events.

### Procedure

Students find POEs straightforward since the technique involves the familiar task of answering direct questions. Only those aspects of the direct questions which are unusual need particular attention.

It is most important initially to ensure that all students understand the nature of the situation about which they are being asked to make a prediction. For the example in Figure 3.1 this involves actually holding the two balls about two metres above the ground and explaining what is required. Allow students to ask questions about the situation in order to have all understand the task before proceeding.

It is crucial to the purposes of POEs to have everyone indicate both their prediction and the reasons they have to support the prediction. This can be either on a prepared sheet, as in Figure 3.1, or of a more open-ended form (that is, have the prediction written in the student's own words). There are two reasons why everyone should complete this before the observation: all students must commit themselves to a position by deciding what knowledge is appropriate to apply and then applying it; and no-one should miss the observation of the event because they are still writing or thinking. Making predictions without recording reasons is rather like ignoring the nature of the links on concept maps: much of the value of the technique for revealing understanding is removed.

When the action occurs, have all students write down their individual observations. As some of our examples will show, there are many occasions for which different students will see different things. If observations are not written at the time they are made, some students will change their observations as a result of hearing what others claim to have seen.

The last step is for students to reconcile any discrepancy between what they predicted and what they observed. Often they find this difficult, and then all you can do is encourage them to consider any possibilities they can think of. That encouragement is important, because the explanations students proffer in this step reveal much about their understanding.

### Examples of POEs

Our examples in this section all involve events which actually occur in front of students. Later in the chapter we give other forms of POEs in which events, such as instances from novels or history, are described to the students. The examples here show something of the range of possible situations, illustrate the forms of student response, and elaborate important issues in using POEs. Most of our examples concern scientific phenomena, because the technique has been used most often in that subject. Readers interested in other subjects should bear with us, however, for POEs can be applied widely.

Our first example involves the situation shown in Figure 3.2. Two beakers containing equal volumes of water and cooking oil are on a single hot plate. In each beaker is a thermometer which reads 0–200°C. The hot plate is turned on, and students are asked to predict how, when the water is boiling, the temperatures of the oil and water will compare. We have found that 13- to 15-year-old Australian students rarely predict correctly that the oil will have a greater temperature. This is revealing about students' lack of readiness to apply everyday experience to science problems, since cooking oil is very common in Australian kitchens. Both of the other two possible predictions are common, with one reason for each case being given frequently. Predictions of a lower temperature for the oil are often supported by the reasoning that 'the oil is not boiling yet', while predictions of equal temperature are usually supported with the fact that both beakers have been heated on the same hot plate for the same time (an 'equal heat input' argument). In both cases students are applying ideas other than those the teacher would expect in order to make their prediction. Merely asking students to explain why the oil is hotter would not allow this.

In this POE, the observation of higher temperature for the oil is straightforward and uncontroversial. In our experience there are occasional mutterings about inadequate thermometers, but these are not serious approaches to the problem of reconciling conflict in prediction and observation. Some students will apply something of what they have learned about the difference between heat and temperature and the differences between substances in absorption and retention of heat energy. Unfortunately the number doing this is less than we, as teachers, would hope for.

The second example of a POE provides a stark illustration of the problems of observing in some cases. It is also an example which requires a much larger time scale for completion. We begin with a large glass jar with a tight fitting lid. A piece of rotting liver is placed in the jar, which is then sealed not only by screwing on the lid but also made gas-tight by dipping the lid in wax. The jar is then placed on the balance. Students are asked to predict the relative weight of the jar (less, same, greater) when the liver has rotted considerably. A time

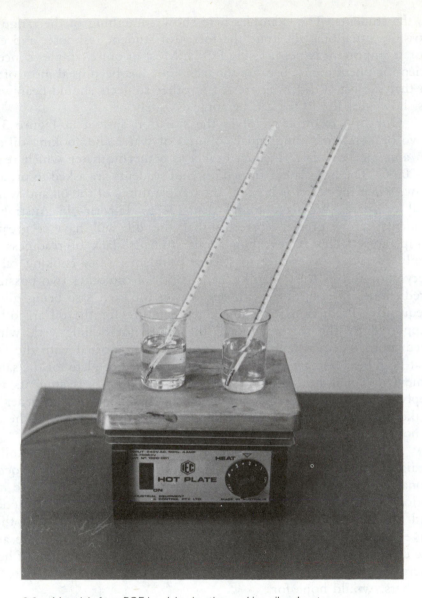

*Figure 3.2: Materials for a POE involving heating cooking oil and water*

interval of about two weeks is appropriate. By far the most common prediction among students who have been taught about conservation of mass is that the weight of the jar will be less after two weeks. The supporting reasons for this prediction usually revolve around the notion that rotting involves disappearing. Some argue, in support of the same prediction, that gases have no weight. Provided the seal on the jar is gas–tight, then the observation of equal weight is undisputed. Some students will, however, use this observation to argue that it is clear that air has indeed got into the jar. That is, some students reconcile conflicting observation and prediction by interpreting the observation in a quite different manner from us. The theory-related aspects of observation are also well illustrated by other POE examples. Before turning to some of them, it is interesting to look at the rotting liver POE in another way. One conclusion which can validly be drawn from the continuation of the common prediction of less weight and the subsequent common rationalization of the conflicting observation has to do with teaching. This example shows clearly the fundamental importance of conservation of atoms to an interpretation of this phenomenon. Conservation of mass is merely a consequence of this. Teaching which recognizes this issue is more likely to have students able and willing to apply conservation of mass in interpreting phenomena.

A number of interesting aspects of the effect of belief (or theory) on observations in POEs are found in uses of the bicycle wheel shown in Figure 3.3.

The bicycle wheel can turn freely on its mount. It forms a large pulley, with a bucket of sand and a large block of wood suspended on either side. Our use of such a cumbersome arrangement instead of a laboratory pulley and weights is deliberate. The extent to which you will probe the ways students choose to interpret real phenomena, and the nature of knowledge and mode of reasoning they decide it is appropriate to apply, depend on whether they see the phenomenon as a usual school-based one or as something from the world at large. In other words, using pulleys of the form only ever seen in school laboratories would have made the task very different. Students are more likely to decide to apply school knowledge if the phenomenon is seen as solely a classroom event.

We have run POEs based on the bicycle wheel with physics and science students from age 15 to graduate level. We found the results described here at all of these levels.

One of these POEs involves the bucket of sand and block of wood placed as shown in Figure 3.3, and at rest, but with no-one

Figure 3.3:    *A bicycle wheel serving as a large pulley has been used in a number of POE tasks*

touching them (i.e., in balance). Students are then asked to predict what will happen when a small teaspoon of sand is added to the bucket. Always some predict that the bucket will move down a little, and then come to rest again at a lower position. The reasoning given to support this prediction is usually based on the view that the position of balance is related to the weight of the objects. The concept *equilibrium* is widely used, as in 'it will fall to its new equilibrium'. Other predictions include that the bucket will move down to ground level (usually because of reasoning based in physics) or that there will be no movement (sometimes because of friction, sometimes because the amount of sand added will not be enough to 'overcome inertia'). These latter predictions are less relevant to our present arguments about observations, although the incorrect 'overcoming inertia' logic does get supported by the observation. When the sand is added, neither we nor the majority of watchers see any movement. This is because the additional weight of sand is insufficient, by comparison with the friction present, to cause movement. Many who predicted a small movement to a new stationary position report that they did see movement. Some write that they saw the bucket move a little; occasionally some will observe that 'the bucket moved so little that I could not see it'.

We do not yet understand one intriguing aspect of student responses to this particular POE. This involves the forms of reconciliation given by those who predict a small movement and report observing no movement. Their reconciliations, in our experience, involve at best only asserting that there was insufficient sand added to cause movement. That is, the issue underlying their prediction (that balance position is related to weight of objects) is never explicitly addressed. Our conjecture is that the prediction is more intuitive than based on explicit reasoning.

A related POE illustrates this observation issue in the same way. After completing the teaspoon of sand POE, students are asked to predict what will happen when a small shovel full of sand is added to the bucket. Again some predictions are that the bucket will move down a distance and come to rest at a new balance (or 'equilibrium') position. In this case the observation is uniform across students. The bucket moves downwards, accelerating, until it reaches the floor. The large bulk of those who predict movement to a new balance position reconcile this with their observation by concluding that the bucket reached the floor before it had reached the new balance position. The reconciliation then involves holding to the prediction and interpreting the observation in these terms.

The extreme case of interpreting an observation solely in terms of prediction results in the denial of the observation. This is well illustrated by a further POE with the bicycle wheel. In this example a different bucket of sand and the block of wood are placed at rest on the wheel, in balance and at the same level. The block is then pulled down a metre or so and held while at this new position. Students are asked to predict what will happen when the block is released. The most common prediction is that the block will move back up to its original position. Reasons given in support are often of the balance/equilibrium form described above, sometimes supported by inappropriate use of physics such as 'conservation of potential energy can only be achieved by a return to the initial position'. The observation of no movement on release is made by all. However the clear majority of those who had predicted a return to initial position always reconcile prediction and observation by denying the legitimacy of the observation. Usually this is done by arguing that 'the block was held for too long in the second position' (with some students explicitly expressing the belief that the block has somehow got used to the new position) or that 'there was too much friction' (that is, if the system had less friction the block would have returned).

These several examples show that observation is influenced by existing ideas and beliefs. This is not a function of the POE task, it is a human characteristic. The issue is certainly more obvious with many POE tasks, but only because the task requires elaboration of at least some relevant ideas and beliefs before the observation. When any person makes an observation in any context, existing ideas and beliefs have some effect both on the aspects of the phenomenon that are focussed on and on what is actually seen.

Another feature of the bicycle wheel POEs is that they illustrate how powerful the strategy can be when situations which, at least superficially, appear relatively straightforward are given to quite advanced learners. Our next example also shows this.

Students are shown two domestic electric light globes functioning normally. One is 100 watt, the other 40 watt, so the difference in intensity of light produced is clear. The two globes are then placed in sockets wired in series. Before the arrangement is switched on, students are asked to predict which of the two globes will now appear brighter or whether they will show the same brightness. We have used this POE only with physics graduates. Nearly all predict that the 100 watt globe will glow more brightly than the 40 watt globe, and use physics knowledge to argue the appropriateness of the prediction. The observation is quite clear and accepted by all: the 40 watt shines with a brightness which appears almost normal while the filament in the 100 watt globe takes several seconds to reach only a dull red colour. Reconciliation leads some students to conclude correctly that they did not discriminate appropriately between power and resistance when reasoning out their prediction.

POEs can be used with much younger students. The materials shown in Figure 3.4 can be used to probe both understanding of the concept of volume and ability and willingness to use the concept to interpret a situation. The smaller cube has sides of half the length of the larger cube, a fact which the students must be told. It is also important for the cylinder containing the water to have clear markings. The teacher places the smaller cube in the water, and points out and marks the rise in level of the water. The teacher then asks the students to predict, with reasons, the rise in water level when the second cube is placed in the water. Reasons that 12- and 13-year-olds give for predictions show both a lack of understanding of the effect on volume of doubling the sides of the cube and a failure to use the concept of volume to argue a prediction.

Many well-known demonstrations can be restructured for use as POEs (although, as we discuss below in the section on 'Choosing Examples', not all demonstrations can be so used). Several of Piaget's tasks are valuable as POEs. Aspects of conservation of volume can be probed with the material shown in Figure 3.5. The left hand container in that figure has water in it to the level of the marking. The marking on the right hand container is at the same height. Students are asked to predict, with reasons, the height the water will reach in the right hand container when the water from the other container is poured in. The mark on the right hand container enables the prediction to be in terms of at, above, or below the mark. A second POE can then explore understanding of what will happen when the water now in the second container is poured back into the original container.

In most POE situations some movement or other notable change occurs. That is not always the case; in the example of the bicycle wheel no movement occurred when the spoon of sand was added or when the block was pulled down. Our final example is another instance.

A weight is hung on a spring (or a spring balance) and the extension of the spring noted by all. The arrangement is then put behind a screen or bench at the front of the room. Students are told that the spring will be pulled up at a steady speed, and asked to predict the extension of the spring in terms of more than, less than, or same as when the weight was hanging from the stationary spring. The

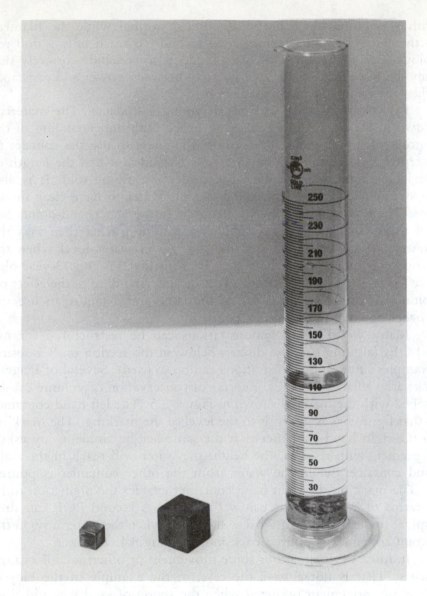

*Figure 3.4: Material for a POE task on volume*

*Figure 3.5:    A Piagetian task used as a POE*

purpose of the screen is to ensure that no observation of the spring can be made until the arrangement is going up at a steady speed. We have found predictions of greater extension to be common among 14- to 17-year-olds (the ages with whom we have used this POE), with the very common supporting reason that something extra is needed to move the weight up.

### Choosing Examples for a POE

The fundamental consideration is to have situations for which students feel able to make a prediction, and for which the prediction is likely to be based on some personal reasoning. Pure guessing is obviously of no value in this context. It would be pointless to use the POE involving light globes, described above, with 12-year-olds. While they could readily guess one of the three alternatives, they could not possibly use any of the physics relevant to the situation to reason out a prediction. It would be most unlikely that they could give any form of reason at all.

It is sensible to select situations that the students are likely to find relevant. If the situation presents a problem that is real to the student, that is very helpful. If the problem is not real to the student, then the materials used to show the POE ought at least be part of the student's world. Hence the bicycle wheel, rather than a pulley, in the examples above; shot put and rubber ball in Figure 3.1 rather than laboratory equipment such as pendulum bobs; cooking oil and water rather than unusual chemicals.

The likely variation in student observations points to the need to make the result of the POE as clear as possible. You cannot assume that all will see the same thing or that all will accept the validity of what they do see. This suggests that the observations should be as direct as is practicable, that meters or other more indirect means of observing should only be used if there is no other possibility.

The range of possible observations influences your choice of format for responses. Predictions can be asked for via a choice of possible responses (as in the falling balls example of Figure 3.1) or in an open response mode (just asking for the prediction to be written). For the falling balls, only three predictions are relevant: shot put arriving first, rubber ball first, same time. It is sensible then to ask students to choose among these three. The same is true for the cooking oil and boiling water. For the pulled-down block on the bicycle wheel, however, it is not so certain that you can think of all the forms that predictions might take — certainly some we have found students make would never have occurred to us — so an open-ended format is better.

Unlike some of the other strategies described in this book, POEs can be used with great frequency. In most contexts the format is not as unusual, nor does the task involve as much time, as some other techniques. Students often react positively to the procedure. The more frequently you use this strategy, however, the more important another issue becomes. In order to illustrate something of the potential of the POE for probing understanding, our examples have been ones for which the observation is unexpected for many students. A concentrated exposure to POEs which always give such unexpected results will have two effects. Students will develop negative attitudes towards the approach, and will begin to predict in terms of 'what unexpected thing might happen' rather than 'what do I reason out will happen'. This second point, the perception of the POE as another form of teacher game of the type so vividly described by John Holt (1967) in his book, *How Children Fail*, is of considerable significance. The way to avoid it is obvious. The more you use POEs the more important it is to include examples where many more students are likely to find their predictions supported by their observations. Such POEs have value, as students still have to mount arguments in support of their predictions before the predictions are confirmed.

## Introducing POE Tasks to Students

Introducing POEs is straightforward. The process of working through a POE example is sufficiently familiar to students that no learning of the process is needed. This is well illustrated by the fact that we have used the bicycle wheel POEs described above successfully with groups of 100 or more who were being exposed to the POE strategy for the first time.

On the first occasion on which you give students a POE, you should be conscious of the need to ensure that all appreciate the situation about which they are to predict, that all write reasons for their predictions, that all write what they have observed, and that all attempt to reconcile any conflict between prediction and observation. The more POEs students undertake, the less the need to reiterate these points.

### Variations and Extensions

We offer two broad groups of variations and extensions: the extension of the strategy into contexts where physical events are not directly observed, and other forms of use with direct observation. We first consider the application of the strategy to unobserved contexts.

#### POEs in Other Contexts

In principle, the POE strategy can be applied to any event or sequence of events — past or present, actual or invented. The examples given below illustrate the range of possible events (and hence contexts) for which this application can reveal student understanding. One variation is whether the task concerns an event that is actually observed or one that is described. Our first example falls between these extremes, in that it uses records of an actual event.

Figure 3.6 shows three weather maps taken from a newspaper on successive days, and a blank map. Students are asked to use the three given maps to predict the map for the next (fourth) day, and to show their prediction by drawing it on the blank map. Reasons for the prediction are also asked for. For the observation component of the task the students are given the actual fourth day weather map as it appeared, and are asked to describe what they see in this information. The reconciliation task is as before, although, as we suggested in our earlier discussions of observation, the complexity of the prediction and observation in this case will mean that students will often over-look features of the observation that are at odds with their predictions. This possibility can be reduced by changing the prediction task, and thus giving a different POE, to 'Give a one sentence weather prediction for (say) Melbourne on the fourth day'. In this case the observation will be a one-line description, taken from the actual newspaper report, of what the weather was on that day. Other variations in the prediction question which might be used are probably obvious. In some cases these will vary according to the issues of importance in reporting the weather in particular locations. For example, it is common in the United Kingdom for newspapers to report the number of hours of sunshine at various locations. Since amount of sunshine is then more likely to be a meaningful idea to UK students, weather maps could be used with the prediction task being 'Predict the number of hours of sunshine in (say) Leeds on the fourth day, and give your reasons'. The observation is then the newspaper record of the number of hours of sunshine on that day.

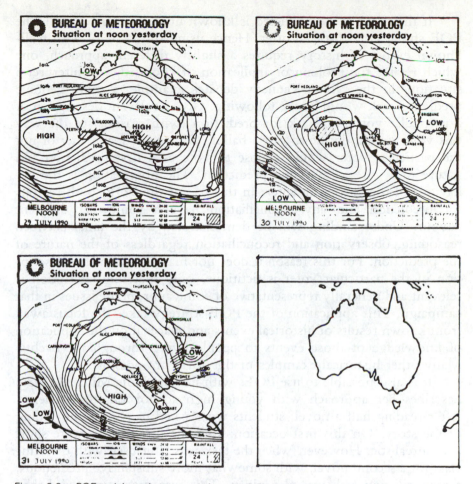

*Figure 3.6: POE task based on successive weather maps*

In this use of weather maps, actual events which have previously occurred provide a form of indirect observation. Historical events and sequences are another form of indirect observation, but with another potential problem. Consider the following example. We conject that a powerful probe of the ideas and reasoning of older students about relations between the media and politics would be to show parts of the televised Nixon-Kennedy debates in the US presidential election of 1960, and to ask for a prediction of the result. The major difficulty is that most would know the result and their predictions will reflect this knowledge. Of even greater importance is that the students will then use the result (taken as the prediction) to select ideas, beliefs or reasoning to justify the result. The process becomes OPE rather than POE.

If the event to be predicted is known unambiguously to all, the POE strategy has little to offer. Hence using the strategy with well-known events of history requires a slightly different approach, one which retains the probing of application of knowledge to interpret a situation. In the Nixon–Kennedy debates example, a more genuine prediction task would be the following. Give a relevant description of a particular voter, and ask for prediction (with reasons) of the way this voter would decide to cast a ballot. Or, perhaps, whether or not the particular voter would choose to vote as a first prediction and nature of a vote as a second prediction. The observation is the behaviour of the particular voter. In this use of the POE, both reasons for prediction and any reconciliation have a somewhat different flavour. Understanding will be demonstrated by the links between reasoning, observation and reconciliation regardless of the nature of the prediction. For this reason it does not matter at all if the description of the particular voter is fictitious, only that the description is relevant and generally representative of some appropriate issues in that campaign. This application of the POE strategy takes the focus away from known results of historical events and places it on the application of knowledge of those events to people living through the events. Many other historical examples of this form are possible.

It is also possible to use POEs with novels. Judie Mitchell (1986) describes her approach with young high school English students. After reading half a novel, students were asked to predict the ending of the story. On this first occasion, students' predictions were short and unrealistic. However, when the task was later used with the same class for a second novel, with somewhat more substantive predictions, a reconciliation task was also given. This was more structured than the rather open form we advocate for use with actual events, a change appropriate to this more complex context for predictions and observation. The structure involved asking for a comparison of prediction with author's version (a comparison oriented observation), a listing of major differences between the two, and 'Was your version more true to the characters than the author's, in your opinion? Explain your reasons' (Mitchell, 1986, p. 117). Responses indicated that the task led to informed and valuable evaluations of predictions, particularly in terms of the social unreality of many.

When used with novels in this way, the POE task is complex and time–consuming. This no doubt means it can be used less frequently in these contexts, but can have a major impact on learning. The same approach can be applied to narrative film or television, perhaps with even more success because the section of the narrative which is seen before the prediction is more obviously controlled.

Art teachers may use a similar procedure. They can show students a large portion of a painting or drawing, and ask them to predict, by completing the work themselves, how the original artist finished it.

### Other Variations

For the remaining variations we return to observable events, though the first one can be applied to described events as well.

In some POEs the undertaking of a second, related POE, with a change of one significant variable, can reveal much of students' understanding. An example is an extension of the falling balls POE shown in Figure 3.1. When we have used that task with physics graduates, they almost always give appropriate predictions and reasons. When, however, we then repeat the POE using a greater height from which to drop the same two balls (about 10 metres), a different picture emerges. The graduates almost always predict equal times for the two balls to reach the ground. The observation is clear in showing the shot put arrives first. By using both POEs together one can probe the ways knowledge is selected and applied both to a context in which the common physics dictum of 'ignore air resistance' is very approximately reasonable (the 2 metre drop), and one where this dictum is quite unreasonable (the 10 metre drop).

A second variation involves using POEs in laboratory work. This is a helpful way of focussing on the issues seen by the teacher as important, in either normal laboratory exercises or in laboratory-based tests. For example, asking students to predict the general shape of the temperature versus time graph for liquid naphthalene left to cool emphasizes the significant feature of data they then collect about temperature and time for the naphthalene. The observation in the POE becomes the data they are collecting in the laboratory experiment.

### What the Procedure Reveals

The POE technique focusses on understanding of situations. In Chapter 1 we described three processes involved in comprehending situations: selecting relevant aspects of the situation, explaining the situation, predicting developments in the situation. Although prediction is the most obvious of these to be probed by a POE, some information is also given about the others through the demand for reasons in support of the prediction. The reasons invoke both data about the beliefs students see as appropriate to a consideration of the situation, and the form of explanation which is constructed using these beliefs.

Because the situations chosen for the use of a POE often focus on a particular concept, as in so many of our examples in this chapter, then understanding of concepts is also often probed. The ideas and beliefs used to argue a prediction will also often reveal the nature of understanding of single elements of knowledge.

## Scoring of POEs

The ways in which POEs foster a form of interaction with a phenomenon or situation, in particular the reconciliation task which allows a reconsideration of arguments, make POEs particularly suited to diagnostic and formative assessment. In this mode they are powerful learning tools. If they are used in contexts which require scoring, some issues require careful consideration.

Paramount is whether or not to score the observation component of the task. If you score this, and thus judge it as correct or incorrect, in subsequent POEs students are likely to write what they think they were supposed to see rather than what they did see. There are certainly some contexts where assessment of the observation could be justified — in particular if one of the purposes you have in using a POE format is to assess observing skill. We urge caution in this, however, and generally see scoring of the observation as inappropriate.

Scoring can evaluate both the beliefs that students reveal and the quality of their reasoning. You may give some credit to a student who applies relevant knowledge, but whose reasoning is faulty or who overlooks other facts. For example, consider again the falling bodies POE. Here are two justifications we have found among those who predict that the heavier ball will arrive first: 'Air resistance will have a much greater effect on the lighter ball, so the heavier ball will fall much more quickly'; 'If you dropped the balls on your feet, the heavier one would hurt much more because it is travelling faster as it falls'. While both reasonings lead to an inappropriate prediction there are differences. In the first case the reasoning is partly correct, but flawed in two ways: the magnitude of air resistance effects on these two balls is greatly overestimated (as shown by the use of 'much'), and the effects of dropping over such a small distance and using such a poor timing device (the eye) are ignored. In the second case the student has taken an inappropriate piece of knowledge (effect on one's feet) and tried to apply it. There may well be good reasons then for giving some credit to the first reasoning.

We would prefer, if POE tasks must be scored, to give particular weight to how the student reconciles any difference between observation and prediction. A reasoned reconciliation demonstrates good understanding, so should yield a high score even though the initial prediction was wrong.

In determining how much weight they should place on the various parts of the students' responses, scorers should consider the nature of the task. Weather prediction, for example (Figure 3.6), is not an exact science, so it would not be reasonable to penalise an incorrect prediction as much as it might be in a more determined situation such as the two falling balls of Figure 3.1. This comment applies to POEs in history and literature.

## Using POEs in Teaching

In earlier sections we indicated the value of POEs in teaching and learning: using a POE to focus student understanding of a laboratory experiment or using the results of a POE to guide sequencing and presentation of content. Many other positive learning effects can follow from using POEs as teaching and learning strategies, all of which are enhanced by requiring written responses for the component tasks.

Some of these effects revolve around the links between the basic POE procedure and that widely-used teaching strategy, the demonstration. In using a POE approach with a demonstration, several positive outcomes are likely. Firstly the insistence on a written prediction makes it more likely that students will understand the situation involving the demonstration. If they do not, their need to ask is more obvious because of the prediction task. We suggest that, in early use in classrooms, predictions be made anonymously and summaries (e.g., 10 students predicted x) reported back to the class. As well as prediction and reason providing a focus for observation, the commitment involved in deciding on a prediction can have powerful motivation effects. When the observation is contentious, a discussion of it can foster valuable learning. Discussion is even more significant in the reconciliation phase. This requires thoughtful handling, of course, and simply asserting a form of reconciling will often do little to promote understanding among students. It has to be true discussion.

One other aspect of the learning value of POEs is that the tasks can demonstrate to students that they already have ideas of relevance to the topic at hand. While this is the case for most content areas, students often do not realize it. Showing them that they make predictions based on reasoning is a powerful counter.

## Further Reading

The use of POEs in science classrooms is described in GUNSTONE, R.F., MITCHELL, I.J. and the MONASH CHILDREN'S SCIENCE GROUP (1988) 'Two teaching strategies for considering children's science', in *The Yearbook of the International Council of Associations of Science Education*, pp. 1–12. This article also provides references to some research studies that used POEs.

The theory-dependent nature of observation is a critical aspect of POEs. It is well elaborated in DRIVER, R. (1983) *The Pupil as Scientist?* Milton Keynes: Open University Press; and also discussed in GUNSTONE, R.F. and CHAMPAGNE, A.B. (1990) 'Promoting conceptual change in the laboratory', in E. HEGARTY-HAZEL (Ed.) *The Student Laboratory and the Science Curriculum*, London: Routledge.

*Chapter 4*

# Interviews about Instances and Events

An Interview about an Instance or an Event is a conversation that an expert has with one student, focussed by initial questions about situations represented in a series of line diagrams, to check the student's ability to recognise the presence of a concept or the student's interpretation of a natural phenomenon or social occurrence. Figure 4.1 shows some of the drawings and focussing questions used by Osborne (1980) to probe understanding of the concept of *electric current*.

## Purposes of Interviews about Instances and Events

Piaget used this technique, with not only drawings but actual objects and events, to probe young children's constructions of meanings for concepts such as life and for natural phenomena such as the moon appearing to follow one as one walks (Piaget, 1927/1969). Among its most prolific users in recent years are Roger Osborne and John Gilbert (1980), who have used it to study the understandings of primary and secondary school students for concepts in physical science such as work and electric current.

   Although most of the applications, and consequently most of the examples we provide, have been in science, there is no reason why the technique could not be used for any concept, for example justice, fair trade, chord, rhythm, musical key, onomatopoeia, balanced diet, kindness, or democracy, or for any event, such as a scene in a play, an incident in a football match, or a political act.

   An interview about an instance is a deep probe of the student's understanding of a single concept, that checks whether the student can not only recognize whether the concept is present in specific instances but also whether the student can explain his or her decision. The

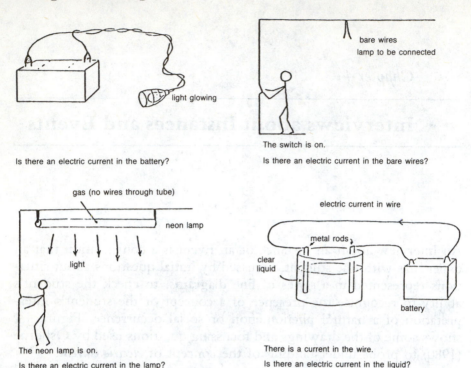

Figure 4.1: *Line drawings and focussing questions used by Osborne (1980) in interviews about electric current*

explanation reveals the quality of the student's understanding. Interviews about events are similarly deep and sharp probes, though the target now is not ability to recognize presence of a concept but ability to explain a phenomenon.

## Procedure

An interview is a conversation that is managed in order to bring out the student's understanding. There is a lot more to it than asking a single question for each diagram such as the focussing question in Figure 4.2.

The interviewer must be ready to follow up the response of the student by asking: Why do you say that? What sort of force? Which way is it acting? Or, if there isn't any force, what will happen to the ball? Will it go on for ever? Since the course of the interview depends on what the student says, the form and sequence of follow-up ques-

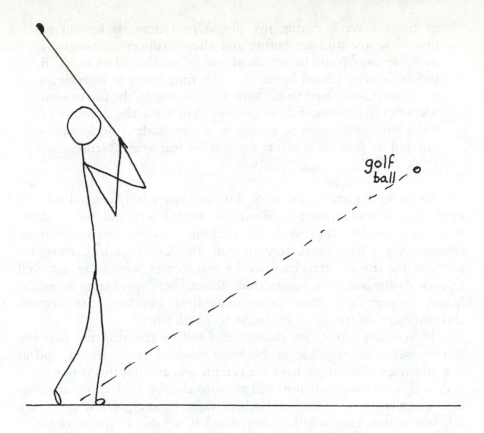

golf
ball

**IS THERE A FORCE ON THE GOLF BALL?**

*Figure 4.2:   Line drawing of instance and focussing question for interview about force*

tions cannot be detailed in advance. The interviewer will, however, have a set of questions in mind for use when appropriate. Knowing what those questions might be is one of the skills of interviewing, a skill that requires practice and familiarity with the subject matter.

An Interview about an Instance or an Event requires from 15 to 30 minutes, and since schools are organised so that students' and teachers' days are full with group activity, one of the most difficult parts of the procedure is to find time and place for it to occur. The experience of an American teacher, Barbara Neureither, suggests that this difficulty is not as severe as one might think:

> How would I find time to do the interviews? It didn't take as
> long as I thought. It only requires about 15 minutes a couple

of times a week during my preparation time. If I want to interview my students before and after a concept is taught, I make arrangements to get them out of another class or do it before or after school hours.... The time spent in interviews is minimal compared to the time I am saving in the classroom. Identifying misconceptions has cut down on the amount of reteaching previously necessary to attain student understanding and to prepare students for further learning. (Neureither, 1990, p. 2)

Once the logistic problem of time and space has been solved, the next issue is the rapport between the interviewer and the student. Rapport must be established, for nothing valuable can come from interviewing a frightened, resentful, or indifferent student. Most reports of the use of interviews are by researchers who were not well known to the students beforehand. Researchers' problems in establishing rapport differ from those of teachers, but both cases require establishment of trust and readiness to speak out.

In research work, we recommend telling the students that the interviewer is interested in problems of teaching and learning, and in the meanings that people have for certain words, that this is not a test and will not be scored, nor will anyone else be told about the student's performance. Since researchers want to analyse responses, we ask our respondents whether they mind if we use a tape recorder; if they do, then the recorder would not be used (in our experience, people never object). Then we tell the student what term the interview is about, and that the idea is to chat about a set of drawings.

This preamble would be modified when the interview is between teacher and student. The teacher might prefer to say that the purpose is to see whether the class has been taught well enough, so he or she wants to check whether the student understands a particular term. Again it might be emphasised that it is not a test, and that no marks hang on it. There should be no need for a tape recorder, since the teacher will form his or her impressions instantly and probably will not have the luxury that a researcher has of being able to reflect at length on the responses.

One of the biggest problems for teachers in interviews is their conflict of roles. Interviewers must not be judgmental, lest they inhibit the responses. It is not easy for a teacher to refrain from comment when the student says something either perceptive or misguided. The teacher needs to follow interviewer's practice of neutral comments such as 'uh-huh' and 'can you tell me more about that?', and restrain from common classroom responses such as 'good', 'correct', and 'no, that's wrong'. Another difficulty for teachers is that they like to teach, so that when a less than satisfactory response is made there is a temptation to put the student right, to explain, to inform. If they do not resist that temptation, the interview ceases to be an interview. It may turn into a positive learning experience for the student, but the original purpose of the session is lost.

Another problem for teachers that researchers do not have is choosing who to interview. The researcher normally picks a student at random, in order to build up an impression of the general level of understanding of an age group or of the common alternative concepts that are held. Teachers' purposes are different; they want to know whether their class has grasped the topic well enough, or whether remedial action is necessary. Since at best they will have time to interview only one or two students, random selection is too chancy for them. Also, they know the students, and the students know them. Should they avoid students with whom they do not get on? Should they pick students whose general achievement is middling, or weak ones? Our inclination would be to choose students whom we regard as achieving a bit below average, since if their understanding is reasonable then we could have some confidence that most of the class have grasped the topic well enough to go on; and we would not be masochists and pick unsympathetic students, but rather ones with whom we would find it easy to establish rapport.

Once rapport is established and the student understands the purpose of the interview, the interviewer presents the first card. The interviewer has at hand several cards, each depicting an instance or event related to the target concept or phenomenon (Figure 4.1). The number of cards will vary with the topic, the age of the students, and the time available. Osborne used from 10 to 20 in most of his work, but teachers may find that fewer are satisfactory. Even one card can help elicit considerable information about the student's understanding.

Suppose the concept being probed is *embarrassment*. When the first card is presented the interviewer asks, 'In your meaning of the word embarrass, is anyone in this situation embarrassed?' The interviewer then probes the reasoning behind the reply, which almost always is either yes or no, by asking 'Why do you say that?', or 'What makes you think that?' The second card is presented only when the conversation about the first produces no further insights into the student's understanding.

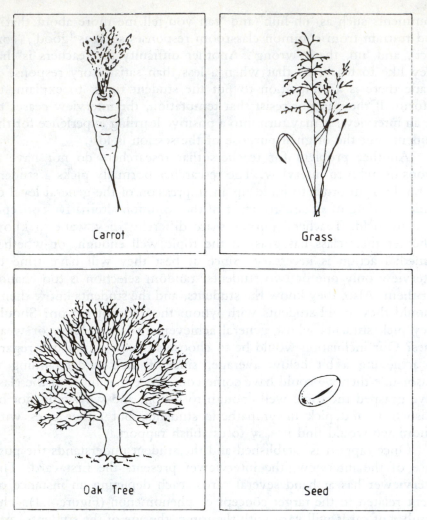

Figure 4.3: *Drawings Bell used to probe student understanding of 'plant' (from Osborne and Freyberg, Learning in Science, Heinemann Education, 1985, p. 5).*

## Examples of Interviews about Instances and Events

Our first five examples draw upon the initial work of Osborne and Gilbert (1980) and the subsequent studies of the *Learning in Science Project* that Osborne directed at the University of Waikato.

Bell (1981; also described in Osborne and Freyberg, 1985) used the drawings of Figure 4.3 to probe students' understandings of *plant*. She asked them, 'In your meaning of the word *plant*, would you say

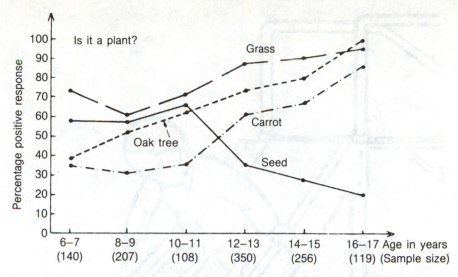

Figure 4.4: *Percentages of students at different ages who rated grass, oak tree, seed and carrot as plants (from Osborne and Freyberg, Learning in Science, Heinemann Education, 1985, p. 6).*

that this is a *plant?*' or, with younger students, 'Would you say that there is a *plant* in this picture?' Then she probed the reasons behind their answers by asking 'Why did you say that?' or 'Why isn't it a plant?'

Figure 4.4 shows a summary of Bell's results. It can be seen that many of the students between 6- and 15-years-old did not class the oak tree as a plant. Their reasons were revealing. One 10-year-old said 'No, it was a plant when it was little, but when it grows up it wasn't, when it became a tree it wasn't.' This student thought of plants as small, newly-planted things, and did not think of them as biologists do as one of the two great kingdoms of living things. The point we emphasise with this example is that although a pencil-and-paper test could have been used to get the summary results of Figure 4.4, the interview revealed the thinking behind the classification that the student made, thinking that must be known in order to design effective teaching for that student and for others in the future.

K. Stead and Osborne (1980, 1981) provide samples of transcripts that demonstrate the course of an interview. One of ten drawings they used in investigating students' notions of *friction* is shown in Figure 4.5.

From an interview with a year 9 student, aged about 15 (I interviewer, S student):

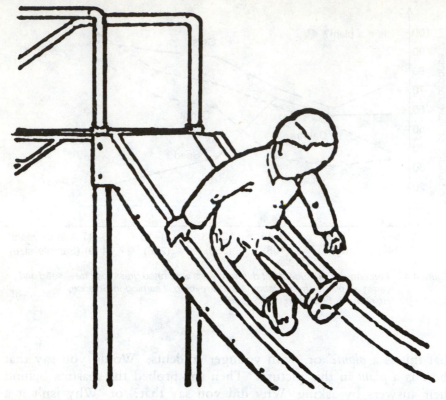

*Figure 4.5:*   *Drawing used by Stead and Osborne (1981) in interview about friction*

**Year 9 student:**

> I:  (card No. 7: boy on slide) ... tell me about that one, Kim.
> S:  Oh it (the friction) makes him slide down so he lands — makes him slide down the slide.
> I:  Sure, so whereabouts is the friction exactly?
> S:  On the ground.
> I:  It's on the ground? So, if it's on the ground, how is it getting to him?
> S:  Oh, it just pulls down like a magnet.

**Year 10 student:**

> I:  Okay, let's take this boy coming down the slide, is there any friction there?
> S:  No.

*I:*  Hum, what about when he hits the bottom?

*S:*  Yeah.

*I:*  So there would be friction when he hits the bottom — would there be much friction?

*S:*  No.

*I:*  Why do you say that?

*S:*  Cos he's sort of coming to a soft landing.

*I:*  He comes to a gradual halt?

*S:*  Yeah.

*I:*  There's only friction when there's a heavy jolt at the end?

*S:*  Yeah.

*I:*  Okay, so if he stood at the top here and fell off (yeah) there'd be a lot of friction when he hit the ground.

*S:*  Yeah. (K. Stead and Osborne, 1980, p. 3)

K. Stead and Osborne note that the year 10 student had a clear though non-scientific concept of friction, which was confirmed when she was asked at the end of the interview for her definition of friction: 'It's when something hits hard together. You get some friction that's soft, but not much, and you have hard, ordinary friction'.

The final transcript shows how the interviewer follows up a common notion that friction is invariably associated with movement. The student is from year 9.

*I:*  We've got a boy coming down a slide here, Reece, any friction in that scene?

*S:*  Yes.

*I:*  Whereabouts.

*S:*  On — down the back of his legs and where he's rubbing against the steel or wood on the slide, and on his hands where he's holding on there.

*I:*  Okay, say he holds on very hard when he gets half-way down and he stops himself, what's that doing to the friction? Is that increasing it or decreasing it?

*S:*  Increasing it.

*I:*  And what say he stops — actually stops moving — what about the friction then?

*S:*  It would decrease it — yeah, decrease it.

*I:*  Would there be any friction when he stopped? When he's holding on very tight?

*S:*  No. (K. Stead and Osborne, 1981, pp. 52–3)

*Figure 4.6:    Drawing used by B. Stead and Osborne (1980) in interviews on light*

The distinction between instances and events is blurred; after all, the cards that are used in interviews about instances often represent events, such as a man hitting a golf ball or a child going down a slide. Nor is the distinction particularly important, since interviews about events will reveal the student's understanding of associated concepts. However, there is some difference in procedure, since in interviews about events the focussing question is not limited to asking whether the drawing illustrates an instance of the target concept. The range of questions can be broader in interviews about events. One of the drawings that B. Stead and Osborne (1980) used to study understanding of the phenomenon of light is shown in Figure 4.6. They asked the students, 'Does the candle make light?' 'What happens to the light?' 'How far does the light from the candle go?' and 'How is it that the person is able to see the candle?' Scientists have a precise view about this phenomenon, and would be in high agreement about the answers. Stead and Osborne, however, found that students often had beliefs that differed from the scientists' view. Some, for instance, said that the light just stays on the candle. Others said it went a foot or so, presumably relating it to the nimbus that is often drawn about a flame.

## First Interview for a Student

As far as we are aware, the numerous research reports on interviews about instances and events concern students who had not been interviewed in that way before. None of the reports mentions any difficulty in getting students to respond. In our own limited experience with the technique, we have found that students are pleased to have someone take an interest in them individually, and are ready to cooperate and can do so without prior training or experience.

Most of the skill in the technique is supplied by the interviewer; the student brings knowledge, which it is the interviewer's task to elicit. Therefore interviews go better as the interviewer gains experience. Probably interviews would go more smoothly if the student had experienced one before and had learned to trust the interviewer, but there is no real difficulty to be anticipated with a student's first interview.

## Variations and Extensions

We give examples of a minor variation in which actual objects or photographs are used instead of line drawings, and a major extension in which the interview becomes the basis for a mass-administered written test.

Replacing drawings with objects may be more of a change than at first appears. Drawings are an abstraction, and may signal to the student that what is wanted is a response from abstract knowledge, where objects call for a response from concrete experience. Drawings and objects may tap different forms of understanding, and reveal inconsistent beliefs that a student holds. Brumby's (1982) study of medical students' understanding of the nature of living things illustrates this. She interviewed them a few days after lectures in which they had been told about cellular structure and the presence of DNA in all living things. She showed them a rock, which was an ambiguous-looking object about the size and shape of a human brain, greenish and pocked with holes. She began the interviews with the focussing question, 'If you were walking along the beach and came across this, how would you go about finding out if it *is* alive, if it *was once* alive but is now dead, or if it has *never been* alive, i.e., non-living?' Of the thirty-two students she interviewed, only one mentioned DNA, and only five described how their decision would depend on tests:

> I'd study its microscopic constitution to see if it was cell-like. If there were cells which were functioning, e.g., were mobile, then I would assume that it *is* alive; if there were cells but no movement then it's dead; if it was crystalline in structure then it's non-living. (Brumby, 1982, p. 109)

Some students planned tests to distinguish between living and non-living only, while twenty-one of the thirty-two relied on unsystematic observation, for instance suggesting that they would prod it to see if it moved, or would put it in water to see if bubbles came out.

Brumby summed up the responses of the students in this and similar tasks:

> The most striking finding in these results is the absence of scientific reasoning by these students.... Science is seen by them as a body of absolute, culture-free knowledge, most of which is recorded in books, or yet to be discovered by experts. Their task as students is to learn it, so they will increasingly 'know' all the answers. Hence they are becoming increasingly skilled at rote-learning, or passively memorizing all the content of their lectures. When confronted with an unfamiliar problem, which by definition requires transfer of a concept learnt in one context, to a different context, many students have difficulty and do not reach a possible solution. (Brumby, 1982, p. 110)

The interview, using an actual object, had tested the students' abilities to apply their knowledge about cells and DNA to a real situation. They might have found it easier to respond to the more abstract situation of a drawing or a verbal description.

An even more powerful probe of understanding involves the student in carrying out a task with objects, while answering questions about reasons for each action. The classic exemplar is Piaget's chemicals task, in which the student has to find which combination of four liquids produces a yellow precipitate (Inhelder and Piaget, 1955/1958). This is a test of ability to plan a systematic cover of all possibilities, and requires no knowledge of chemistry. Practical tasks will, however, often be useful bases for interviews probing understanding of some concept or principle. A simple task that probes understanding of the principle that electricity flows in a circuit requires students to arrange a dry cell, globe, and wire so that the globe lights. It has been used in interviews by Tiberghien and Delacôte (1976), Fredette and Lochhead (1980), and Andersson and Kärrqvist (1979), with students from elementary school to second year college, and has proved to be an effective means of uncovering inappropriate beliefs.

Although interviews are a powerful method for probing understanding, they are not convenient when there are many students to test. Some of their incisiveness can be retained when common conceptions revealed in interviews are used as alternatives in a mass-administered test.

Erickson (1979) used four tasks to uncover the beliefs that children aged from 6 to 13 had about heat and temperature. The tasks were to observe the expansion of liquid in a tube and the action of heat on metal cubes, sugar, butter, and a moth ball; to predict the final temperature when two lots of water were mixed; and to predict the results of and observe heat races in which candles were placed under rods of different materials, along which were pins held by wax beads which would melt and allow the pins to fall. Part of the interviews using these tasks had the form of prediction-observation-explanation that is described in Chapter 3. Analysis of the responses of the 12-year-old children enabled Erickson to identify three main forms of belief about heat and temperature, which he termed the current Kinetic view, the historic but now discarded Caloric view, and a mixed set of ideas — the Children's view. He incorporated these views in an inventory that children answered as a written test. The inventory was completed by 276 students who were tested whole classes at a time, and produced similar insights into their understanding as had the more time-consuming interviews. Erickson asserts that the inventory is suitable for classroom use and can easily be used by teachers to diagnose difficulties of students and to plan teaching sequences.

Another example of the development of a written test from an interview comes from the investigation by Nussbaum and Novak (1976) of young children's concept of the Earth. The original study involved individual interviews, using a mixture of line drawings and a model globe (Figure 4.7). The interviews enabled Nussbaum and Novak to identify five types of notion about the Earth, ranging from one that the Earth is flat and continued infinitely sideways and downwards, to the scientific view. Nussbaum (1979) incorporated these notions in a multiple choice test that he administered individually to a new group of students, who were asked to explain each choice. The test could have been given to a whole class at once.

One further example comes from Bell's interviews on understanding of *plant*, that we referred to earlier in this chapter. One of our doctoral students based a written test on Bell's work, with questions such as 'Is *grass* a plant? Explain your reasoning;' and 'Write why you believe *a carrot* is or is not a plant.' This test was not as sensitive a probe of understanding as the interview, but did allow whole class use.

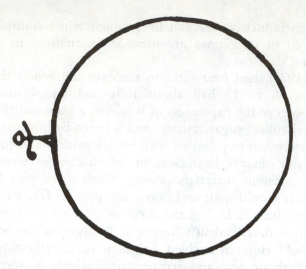

Figure 4.7: *Line drawing used by Nussbaum and Novak (1976) in interviews on concept of the earth*

## What the Procedure Reveals

There has been a revolution in research in science education in the past fifteen years, as interviews and the prediction-observation-explanation probe of Chapter 3 were used for one concept and principle after another to discover that apparently successful learning was often a veneer disguising poor understanding. Interviews are a powerful means of revealing quality of understanding of concepts, principles, and situations. Though their use has been concentrated in science education, there is no reason why they should not be equally useful in all subjects.

When interviews and POEs first began to dig beneath the veneer of rote learning, researchers and teachers tended to laugh in a rather embarrassed way at the unexpected things that students said. They labelled the students' beliefs as misunderstandings or misconceptions. As time passed, it became more widely appreciated that there was a rational, if often mistaken, basis to many of the beliefs, for they could be traced to constructions of reality that the students had made for themselves from experiences they had had before entering the class-room. For instance, students who came into physics classes to learn about Galileo's and Newton's laws of motion were found to adhere to Aristotelian views such as velocity rather than acceleration being proportional to force and hence that if something is moving there must be a force on it. Though not the way that scientists represent the world, this belief is not so inconsistent with observation in a world of friction and air resistance as to cause its holders much trouble in making sense of what they see day to day. Consequently there has been a move away from calling beliefs misconceptions towards the term *alternative conceptions*.

The research on alternative conceptions has emphasised Ausubel's (1968) point that the final state of learning is a combination of prior knowledge and the new information that has been presented in instruction. The research has come up with a surprise, however, that was not foreseen by learning theorists or by experienced teachers: where prior beliefs and instruction are incompatible, it is rare for resolution of contradictions to occur; nor does one proposition win out over the other. Rather, both views are stored in memory. This schizophrenic state of knowledge causes students little trouble, as the teacher's statements are recalled in the context of the classroom and school-type tests and the experience-based self-constructed knowledge in the context of everyday life. The power of interviews is that they can tap the deeper beliefs even though they occur in a school context.

The discovery through interviews that students can hold contradictory beliefs has fuelled interest of researchers and teachers in learning styles. Presumably if students reflected on their knowledge, and were active in checking whether new information was consistent with what they believed, they would discuss and resolve the contradictions. Presence of contradictions indicates shortcomings in learning style. Hence interviews are not only a means of probing understanding of a specific piece of subject matter, but reveal the quality of a student's general style of learning.

## Scoring of Interviews about Instances and Events

Although a score could be given to a student for performance in an interview, there are two reasons why one will rarely do that. First, it is unlikely that a teacher will have time to interview all the students in a class, and marks lose much of their point when they cannot be compared. Second, the conduct of an interview depends on trust; the student must be willing to respond freely without having to weigh each word for its effect on the score. Once students know that marks are being given, they are less willing to 'think aloud'. Therefore we provide no guide to the scoring of interviews about instances and events.

### Using Interviews in Teaching

The revelation by interviews and prediction–observation–explanation of widespread and persistent alternative conceptions is having a growing influence on the teaching of science. As they come to be used in other subjects they are likely to influence their teaching also.

Teachers and curriculum designers have always known that students neither learn all nor understand fully all that they are taught, but interviews have surprised them over the extent to which alternative beliefs exist and persist in the face of contrary instruction. This has led to recognition that teaching is more than the simple presentation and clear explanation of facts; the relation between the facts and prior beliefs must be considered. That consideration turns out to be far from simple. Before students will consider new propositions, Posner, Strike, Hewson and Gertzog (1982) argue that they must be dissatisfied with their old beliefs and find the new propositions intelligible, plausible, and fruitful.

Intelligibility and plausibility are easy targets for a competent teacher, but dissatisfaction and fruitfulness are difficult. Dissatisfaction is not secured by the teacher telling the students that they are wrong. All that happens then is that they learn the teacher's view as an addition to their own, even if they are incompatible. In the long run, once students leave school and examinations behind, they can discard the teacher's view and the schooling will have had no lasting effect. Nor is fruitfulness, the other side of the dissatisfaction coin, simple to foster. It cannot be produced simply by telling the students that 'you will need this next year' or 'you will need this for the examination', for all that that does is encourage temporary storage of the information, which can be forgotten as soon as the need has passed. Also, such exhortations restrict the value of the knowledge to the context of school; they do not show how it would be fruitful in life outside school now and in the years to come.

Both dissatisfaction and fruitfulness will require different forms of teaching than are currently dominant. Practical possibilities for those forms are described by White (1988), Osborne and Freyberg (1985), Baird and Mitchell (1986), Brown (1980), and Paris, Saarnio and Cross (1986). All involve the principle that students must take more responsibility for their learning, and become more purposeful and reflective. Of these many practical ways, we choose to mention here the promotion of question-asking by students. Analyses of classroom interactions by Flanders (1970) and later researchers have found that teachers initiate almost all sequences in class and do about two-thirds of the talking; students not only say little, but what they do say is usually a response to a command or question from the teacher. They do not ask questions, nor is there any sense of a conversation such as occurs in an interview. We advocate the promotion of question–asking by students, because it will make them reflect on their beliefs and evaluate new information, and because it will introduce to the classroom some of the quality of an interview; the questions the students ask will reveal more of their understanding. Chapter 10 expands this.

Interviews not only reveal alternative conceptions, they also provide positions for debates that can resolve opposing views. We have seen vigorous, even vehement, yet productive arguments in secondary school classes when a teacher has put forward opposing statements gained from interviews, and has asked students which view they support.

## Further Reading

Any further reading about interviews about instances and events should begin with OSBORNE, R. and FREYBERG, P. (1985) *Learning in Science: The Implications of Children's Science*, Auckland: Heinemann. The authors describe probes, and give a guide to interviewing practice together with examples of interview schedules and pencil-and-paper formats. The book contains a useful list of references to research studies that used interviews, and discusses the implications of the research for teaching.

The chapter by GILBERT, J.K., WATTS, D.M. and OSBORNE, R.J. in L.H.T. WEST and A.L. PINES (Eds) (1985) *Cognitive Structure and Conceptual Change*, Orlando, Fl: Academic Press describes ways of generating instances or events for interviews.

Interviews can provide statements that classes debate in interpretative discussions, and so help students resolve contradictions in their thinking and secure better understanding. Interpretative discussions are described in BARNES, D.R. (1976) *From Communication to Curriculum*, Harmondsworth: Penguin Books.

Chapter 5

# Interviews about Concepts

An interview about a concept is a conversation designed to bring out the knowledge that a person has about the concept. Some interviewers may restrict knowledge to facts, but we recommend extending them to beliefs and opinions, strings, images, episodes, and even intellectual and motor skills if these are relevant to the concept.

Here is a verbatim transcript of an interview with a 22-year-old university graduate:

(*Interviewer*):   We're trying to get an idea of all the ideas and facts people have associated with one particular concept. So, I'm going to ask you a series of questions, some of them very broad and others more specific about a particular concept. The concept is eucalypts. What can you tell me about eucalypts?

(*Respondent*):   Ah — trees — gum trees — ah — koala bears eat the leaves of gum trees — they're like eucalypts. Eucalyptus oil for sore muscles, I suppose. That's it. Mouthwash, I suppose. Lollies.

I:   Any personal experiences? . . . Have you used eucalyptus oil? Or . . .?

R:   No. I've licked throat lollies. Gum leaves — I've put them in my mouth.

I:   Any mental pictures you've got in your mind?

R:   Just that it's a tree in Australia.

I:   Apart from the things you've mentioned, there's a few more specific things — anything you'd like to add about types of eucalypt?

R:   No.

I:   Names of different sorts?

*R:* I don't know any names.

*I:* That's not uncommon. Leaves of eucalypts?

*R:* They're different. Some are narrow and sort of curvey. They're all curvey, I suppose. Some eucalyptus trees are taller than others. That's about it.

*I:* Uh huh. The roots of eucalypts?

*R:* No — can't remember a thing about that.

*I:* Flowers of eucalypts?

*R:* (unintelligible) They're sort of hard (mumbles) shells.

*I:* Uh huh. Got any mental pictures or personal experiences about those things?

*R:* I used to drill a hole through them, stick a feather in, throw it up, watch it come down.

*I:* Uh huh, a pretty good pastime, I remember it well.

*R:* Yes.

*I:* The branches of eucalypts?

*R:* Usually white, usually the skin is peeled off. Ummm ...

*I:* The bark of eucalypts?

*R:* They're pretty smooth.

*I:* Uh huh.

*R:* Some of them are. Um. That's it.

*I:* Uh huh. The sap of eucalypts?

*R:* No.

*I:* Anything about fires and eucalypts?

*R:* I suppose they're ... no.

*I:* No personal experiences or mental pictures?

*R:* When you burn eucalyptus leaves it smells nice, I suppose.

*I:* Very definitely a personal experience — if you try hard you can even remember what it smells like.

*R:* Yes.

*I:* Lovely. One of these days I'm going to install a eucalyptus fireplace in this room. Just to finish with, here are a number of specific terms that might somehow be connected with eucalypts. Is there anything you would like to add about any of these? Gums and boxes.

*R:* Gums and boxes?

*I:* Gum trees and box trees.

*R:* The same.

*I:* Uh huh.

*R:* Are eucalypts basically.

*I:* Anything else you would like to add about eucalyptus oil?

*R:* No.

I:  Uh huh. KDHW.
R:  What's that?
I:  Kiln dried hardwood.
R:  Um — it's not eucalypt.
I:  Uh huh. Hans Heysen.
R:  Is that a tree?
I:  No, it's a man.
R:  I've never heard of him.
I:  He paints gum trees.
R:  Oh.
I:  That's all right, it's just in case I was triggering something there. Anything else about koalas?
R:  They're drugged from the eucalyptus. They seem sleepy most of the time.
I:  Uh huh. Cumberland Valley.
R:  Nothing.
I:  1939.
R:  I wasn't born then.
I:  That's one for us old fogeys. There was a big bush fire in 1939.
R:  I was just going to say bush fire but I was probably guessing.
I:  Mallee roots.
R:  No.
I:  Anything else about eucalypts?
R:  They're fast growing and store a lot of water. And are pretty nice trees.
I:  Thanks very much.

The interviewer was known to the interviewee, so only a brief time was spent in establishing rapport. Presumably, teachers would normally have formed easy relations with their students, and would not need more than a sentence or two to get to the business of the interview. However, when the two people are not known to each other the interviewer may need to chat for some time until the interviewee is relaxed and so able to recall information without strain.

The interview was designed to elicit propositions, images, and episodes, so there were three main questions: What can you tell me about gum trees, which calls for propositions; What mental pictures do you have, asking for images; and What experiences have you had, for episodes. The interviewer has kept asking about each sort until the interviewee started to show strain in recall, then moved on to the next sort.

Note also that the interview moved from being open and general to closed and specific. It was open to begin with because the interviewee can have knowledge that the interviewer lacks or is even unaware could exist, and has to be given a chance to express it. The later specific questions act as stimuli for the recall of knowledge that the interviewee has but has failed to recall for the moment. Of course the interviewee might have other knowledge that has not been recalled and that the specific questions do not stimulate, but that possibility can never be eradicated. The interviewer must choose the questions to cover as broad a sweep of the concept as possible.

## Purposes of Interviews about Concepts

A concept was defined in Chapter 1 as the total set of knowledge that a person associates with a label, and several types of knowledge were discriminated — propositions, strings, images, episodes, and intellectual and motor skills. Understanding of the concept is a function of the set of knowledge. Broadly, understanding improves as the amount of knowledge increases and as the various elements in it become more intensively linked with each other. The quality of the understanding will depend on the proportions of the different types of knowledge. Given this description, interview is the most direct method, among all the probes, of assessing a person's understanding. Its purpose is to bring forth as much as possible of what the person knows about the concept, for that knowledge to be analysed to yield measures or impressions of the person's understanding.

The analysis will depend on what the interviewer (or teacher) thinks is important. Summing up the results of an interview is like describing a complex object such as a house. The points one focusses on vary with one's purpose, so one could mention the house's floor area, number of rooms, material of construction, colours, number of windows, type of floor covering, orientation, and so forth. So with an interview one could consider the extent of the person's knowledge, its accuracy, its interlinking, and its variety of types. The purpose of an interview is to provide so complete a representation of the person's knowledge that any dimension of understanding can be assessed.

## Procedure

The procedure in an interview is deceptively simple. The two people sit comfortably in a secluded spot, safe from interruptions, and one asks questions and the other responds. Perhaps a tape recorder is used, though some experienced interviewers prefer to take their own notes because they believe that recorders inhibit interviewees while note-taking provides assurance that what they are saying is valued by the interviewer.

The simplicity is deceptive because running an interview requires sensitivity and skill. The interviewer has to keep the respondent calm and co-operative. Consequently the interview will begin normally with a period of informal and apparently inconsequential chat, during which the purpose and procedure will be described. If a tape recorder is to be used, the interviewer will ask whether the respondent minds about it, and if permission to use it is given, will turn it on in this introductory period rather than at the commencement of the questioning.

The interviewer will have a list of questions. In order that the interview remains informal and productive, the questions are not read out nor is their sequence immutable. The interviewer is free to vary their form a little, and to ask them in any order that seems convenient. It is then a good procedure to mark them off unobtrusively, so that a check near the end of the interview can reveal whether any remain to be asked.

One of the skills in interviewing is judging when to move on to the next question. If the questions are asked too rapidly, the respondent may become flustered, or could become unresponsive since it would appear that further things he or she had to say were not valued. Excessive pauses, on the other hand, may be embarrassing and again fluster respondents as they conclude that they are expected to know more and so must be performing poorly. In our experience, if an error is made it is less serious for the questions to come slowly than when they are rushed.

Another skill is for the interviewer to say enough to keep the respondent talking, without being judgmental. Of course it would be an appallingly bad interviewer who said things like 'Wrong! How can you think that?', but it is just as judgmental (though not as inhibiting) to say 'Good, good. That's correct'. The interviewee will then start looking for judgement on every statement, and will speak to please the interviewer rather than make a relatively independent response. It is better for the interviewer to be encouraging but non-committal, employing words and sounds such as yes, can you tell me any more?, uh huh, thank you, do you remember anything else? Sometimes an unusual response will leave the interviewer uncertain about how to respond. Repeating the statement in a neutral tone may allow unthreatening time for thought by both parties, and often stimulates the interviewee to elaborate the point.

Not being judgmental is one key principle. Another is for the interviewer to say the minimum possible, just sufficient to keep the interview moving.

An even more serious error than being judgmental would be for the interviewer to teach during the interview. That would have an inhibiting effect and destroy the purpose. It is not easy for teachers to avoid this error when interviewing their own pupils. Indeed, the conflict of roles between teaching and interviewing may be one reason why teachers have not used interviews as much as they could.

The interviewer needs to be alert to signals that the respondent has had enough. These signals will often be non-verbal, twisting in the chair, facial expressions of boredom or aggression, tenseness, hand movements. If reasonable rapport exists, interviewees will usually respond positively to statements such as 'I know you must be getting tired of this, but do you mind if I ask you just one or two more things?' Eventually, though, the interview has to close. We usually end by asking, 'Is there anything else that you have thought of?', then thanking the interviewee for helping.

What happens next depends on the use that is to be made of the interview. Teachers might find that they need go no further, since they could have found out all they want to know about their students' understanding. However, further processing of the interview may produce subtle insights. Researchers would in any case want to study more intensively what the respondents said.

Some people can analyse interviews by listening to recordings, but most will find it easier to work from a transcript. In our own work we have not made verbatim transcripts; instead we have gone directly to a reworded set of discrete elements of knowledge. Figure 5.1 shows the reworded set derived from the sample interview at the beginning of this chapter. Hesitations and false starts and interjections from the interviewer are excluded from the reworded set, so some information has been discarded. Although we are aware of that, it does not worry us since we found that the discarded information told us little about understanding. That is not to say that it would not tell other people something of value to them — the procedure of processing will depend on the purpose and on the model of understanding that the interviewer has.

P: Proposition      I: Image      E: Episode

(P)    Eucalypts are gum trees.
(P)    Koala bears eat the leaves of gum trees.
(P)    Eucalyptus oil is used for sore muscles.
(P)    Eucalyptus is used in mouthwash.
(P)    Eucalyptus is used in lollies.
(E)    I've licked throat lollies.
(E)    I've put gum leaves in my mouth.
(I?P?)   Eucalypts are trees in Australia.
(P)    Some eucalypt leaves are narrow.
(P)    All eucalypt leaves are curvey.
(P)    Some eucalypt trees are taller than others.
(P)    Eucalypt flowers are hard.
(E)    I drilled a hole in eucalypt flowers, stuck a feather in them and threw it up and watched it fall.
(P)    Branches of eucalypts are usually white.
(P)    Usually the skin is peeled off the branches of eucalypts.
(P)    Eucalypts have smooth bark.
(I?E?)   When you burn eucalypt leaves it smells nice.
(P)    Gum trees and box trees are the same thing.
(P)    Koalas are drugged by eucalyptus.
(P)    Koalas are sleepy most of the time.
(P)    Eucalypts grow fast.
(P)    Eucalypts are pretty nice trees.

*Figure 5.1:*    *Reworded set of propositions, images and episodes derived from transcript of interview*

We find the rewording of an interview into a form such as that in Figure 5.1 useful, because our model of memory includes images and episodes and so forth, and because our notion of understanding is that its quality depends on the mix of the different sorts of element of memory and how well inter-related they are for the person. Therefore we like to look at how many propositions the person recalls, and how many images and episodes; we count the number of times the person brings in concepts from other fields of knowledge; and we analyse the pattern of linkings between the elements. We would find it difficult to do those things straight from a hearing of the tape or even from a verbatim transcript.

A reworded set is useful as a permanent record of the interview, and as the basis for scoring. It is much easier to compare the responses of two people by looking at the reworded sets than by listening to their tapes or reading their verbatim transcripts, and it is much easier to use them when considering what score to place on the interview. This is particularly true when the comparison or score involves several dimensions, which as we said earlier when using the analogy of describing a house will most often be the case.

### A Respondent's First Interview

Hardly any of the people we have interviewed, from 11-year-olds to adults, had ever been asked before to tell someone what they knew about a concept. Their experience in school and university had been limited to answering specific questions. Their closest parallel to the marshalling of knowledge required in an interview was constructing an essay or doing a project. Despite the novelty of an interview, we have never found any respondents who could not cope. None appeared inhibited or even nervous. The one-to-one conversation is not threatening.

The interviewer must be careful to keep the situation supportive, of course. Non-verbal signals are as important as verbal. We recommend that there be no physical barrier between interviewer and respondent, such as a table or desk. Both people should be on similar chairs, and close together. We find it more comforting to the interviewee if the chairs do not face each other directly, but are at a slight angle. Facial expression is important. The interviewer needs to look interested, which may not be easy if a large number of people has already been interviewed. Sometimes, too, it is not easy to keep surprise or doubt out of one's face. However, it needs to be done in order to keep the interview flowing and unbiased. The rule throughout is to be supportive but not judgmental, either positively or negatively.

### What the Procedure Reveals

Interviews are so flexible there is really no limit to what they can reveal. They can be combined with any of the other probes — concept maps, relational diagrams, word association, and the rest — to dig deeper and deeper into the person's knowledge. They can be open, inviting the person to tell all that is known about the concept, or specific, in which direct questions are asked. It is simple to move back and forth between generality and specificity. They can be directed at any of the different forms of knowledge — facts, opinions, images, episodes. Assessments can be made from them of the quality of the understanding, on many dimensions. Indeed, an interview is the most powerful of probes.

In our first extensive use of interviews about concepts we asked science graduates first about electric current and then about gum trees (White and Gunstone, 1980). The interviews were so powerful a probe that we found out more about the quality of the graduates' understanding than was good for our peace of mind — we were astonished at the poverty of understanding that many revealed. For instance, the interviews were carried out on a campus that is dominated by gum trees, all of which flower for considerable periods. When we asked the graduates to tell us what they knew about the flowers on gum trees, about half expressed surprise that they flowered at all. The knowledge that they had about gum trees was in many cases scanty, and tended to have been acquired from books rather than experience. There were exceptions, people who had built up substantial understanding by integrating book learning with observation.

We were surprised also by the proportion of the graduates with poor recall of knowledge about electricity, which is a topic that had been part of their studies for several years at school and again at university. As the oldest of the graduates was 27 and had hardly had time to forget well-learned information, we regarded recall of as few as 29 total elements of knowledge as meagre, demonstrating poor understanding. The greatest number of elements for electric current was 145, showing that those with weaker understanding were well down.

It could be argued that it is unreasonable to expect people to recall much about a topic chosen without warning from the universe of knowledge. However, we would have expected young science graduates to recall a lot about the important topic of electricity, and it concerns us that so many had been untouched by the spirit of science that they were unobservant enough not to have seen flowers on the gum trees that they passed every day. The interview probed their understanding only too well. It not only revealed the quality of their understanding, but also told us about their learning styles. Because of their power, interviews are a technique that teachers should use despite their difficulties.

## Scoring of Interviews about Concepts

The scoring of an interview will depend on the interviewer's purpose and model of understanding. The interviewer might require only a single, global estimate of the quality of understanding, or might want measures on several dimensions. Since our purpose and model are unlikely to be identical with everyone else's, the scoring procedure that we have used in our work (White and Gunstone, 1980) is pre-

**Propositions**
1  Electric current is charged particles moving through a medium of some sort.
2  Electric current goes faster through a conductor.
3  Metal is a good conductor.
4  An ionic solid is a good conductor.
5  Electric current comes out of plugs.
6  I associate charge with atoms and ions.
7  Protons have positive charge.
8  Electrons have negative charge.
9  Potential difference is the difference of electric charge in two different areas.
10  Battery is a thing that goes in a car.
11  Battery is a thing you stick in a torch.
12  Battery has a positive terminal and a negative terminal.
13  Battery is usually a square thing.
14  Insulators are used to prevent electric current getting from one place to another.
15  AC and DC have something to do with electric current.
16  Ohm's Law has an I in there and a V.
17  Ohm's Law has something to do with electricity.
18  Electric current is continuous.
19  Electric current turns on lights.
20  Water has something to do with making electric current.
21  Yallourn power station makes electric current.
22  Electric current is used in the home.
23  Electric current is used for light.
24  Electric current is used to move things in motors.
25  DC stands for direct current.
26  Amp had something to do with electric current.
27  Amp was French.

**Images**
1  I see electric current as little electrons running through.
2  I think of electrons as an e with a negative at the top.
3  I visualise something out of Stove & Phillips — some diagram showing electrons running through.
4  Resistance is a little squiggly thing.

**Episodes**
1  I've plugged in plugs.
2  I used batteries on the teaching round to do an experiment in chemistry.
3  When the car battery has been flat I've had to put jumper leads on it — twice.
4  I suppose we did something with resistances in 5th form.

*Figure 5.2:   Propositions, images and episodes from an interview with a science graduate*

sented only as an example. Other teachers and researchers will develop their own procedures.

We think that a number of facets of knowledge are involved in understanding. For one thing, we take the fairly obvious position that the more the person knows about a concept, the better the understanding. Of course, someone might believe lots of propositions that turn out to be false, but on balance it is sensible to count the number of elements in the reworded set and use this as one measure of understanding, the *extent* of knowledge. For the example of Figure 5.2, the *extent* score is 35.

The accuracy of the propositions can be taken into account in a second measure, the proportion of the statements that are in *accord with reality or authority*. In the sample set of Figure 5.2, there are 27 propositions, of which numbers 2, 4, and 9 have been marked wrong. The respondent's score on *accord*, therefore, is 24/27 × 100 = 89.

Some statements are not wrong, but are so vague that they reflect a lesser quality of understanding than clear-cut, precise statements do. Therefore we mark each proposition as precise or vague, and give the interview a score on the dimension of *precision* by working out the percentage of precise statements. For the example of Figure 5.2, five (nos. 15, 16, 17, 20 and 26) of the 27 propositions are marked not precise, so that the *precision* score is 22/27 × 100 = 81.

For some purposes one might want to know not only how much the person knows and how accurate and precise the knowledge is, but also whether any contradictory statements are expressed. The respondent might, for instance, at one point say that Belem is in Brazil and at another that it is in Mexico. We have not observed contradictions often, but where they occur they are important indicators of a failure to reflect on and integrate knowledge. As integration is a key quality of understanding, we have scored reworded sets from interviews for *internal consistency*, calculating an index equal to (1 — no. of contradictory propositions/total no. of propositions) × 100. The example in Figure 5.2 contains no contradictions, so its index has the value 100.

We have been interested to find that people differ in propensities to report propositions, images and episodes. The difference reflects a variation in learning style that should be more widely appreciated by teachers and researchers. Some people give a mix of all three sorts of memory element, but others are consistent in preferring to concentrate on one form. We chose electric current and gum trees as the subjects for our interviews with science graduates because we could not imagine much overlap between those topics, and that would allow consistencies in preferences to emerge. One man stood out because his understanding was entirely propositional. He knew a lot, especially about electricity, but we could not get him to describe any images or episodes. When the interviewer asked 'Have you had any experiences involving electric current?' he replied, 'No', and immediately burst forth with more facts. In sharp contrast was another man who could not recall many of the facts he had once known but who was full of episodes. He told us how he had been working on his car, and was listening to the engine by placing a metal rod between the engine block and his ear, when he inadvertently let the rod touch the high tension cap on a spark plug and got a shock in his ear. He had rewired his house, by accident he had fused the wires on his motorbike to the fuel tank, he had seen lightning strike a tree.

The two men had understandings of electric current of very different quality. Therefore we score interviews for the proportions of the total number of elements that are propositions, images and elements. In the example of Figure 5.2 there are 35 statements in all, of which 27 are propositions, 4 images, and 4 episodes. These can be turned into percentages to give a set of scores on a dimension of *variety of types of element*. The scores could be extended to include intellectual and motor skills and strings, if desired.

We also are interested in the number of times the respondent brings in concepts that we would judge as not integrally related to the target concept. Koestler (1964) described creative people as those who could see connections between topics that for most people are unrelated. Therefore an index of externality, equal to the percentage of propositions involving concepts that are not central to the target concept, represents an important dimension of understanding. In Figure 5.2, we judge that the concepts car, torch, water, home and French are external to the topic of electric current, as against conductor, charge, electrons, insulators and so on, which we see as internal. The external concepts figure in 5 of the 27 propositions, so the *externality* score is $5/27 \times 100 = 19$.

A person could report lots of external associations, but in such a disjointed manner that the impression would be of an unintegrated knowledge, a collection of almost random facts that have not been reflected upon and built into a coherent and well-understood body of knowledge. Therefore we are keen to inspect the structure of the person's knowledge by looking at the pattern of associations between the various statements. Are they inter-linked, or are they isolated, individual elements? The more extensive the interlinking, the better the understanding.

The degree of interlinking in a reworded set of statements can be determined roughly by inspection, which may suffice for many purposes. A more detailed analysis involves constructing a matrix of the number of terms pairs of statements have in common. Statements 15 and 25 of Figure 5.2 both contain the terms DC and electric current, so have two links. The matrix of associations for the Figure 5.2 set is shown in Figure 5.3. From that matrix a map of associations has been drawn in Figure 5.4, together with a map for another person's set. We interpret the maps as showing that the second one depicts a richer pattern of linking, a much better integrated knowledge of the concept,

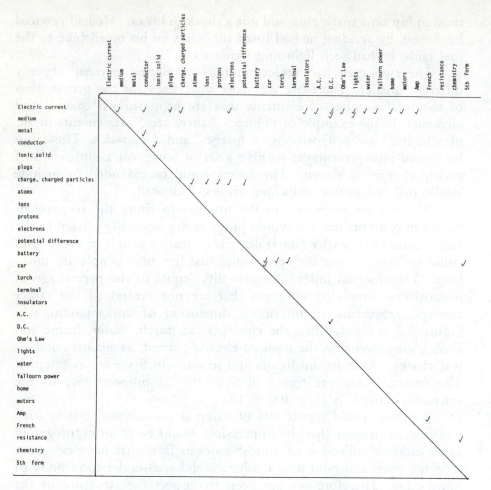

Figure 5.3:  *Matrix of association between concepts in interview protocol of Figure 5.2*

and consequently a better understanding than the map generated from the matrix for the protocol of Figure 5.2.

If necessary, it should be simple to generate a summary figure from the matrix, such as the total number of links or the average number per statement, to give a score on this dimension of *shape* of understanding. In our research we have not needed to do that, preferring to inspect the maps and infer the quality of understanding from them.

The final dimension that we will describe, though by no means the last that other people might be interested in, cannot be determined from transcripts or reworded sets. It is an impression that can be

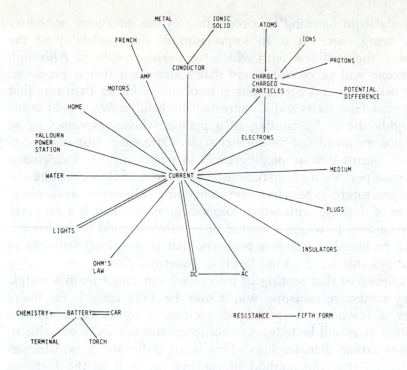

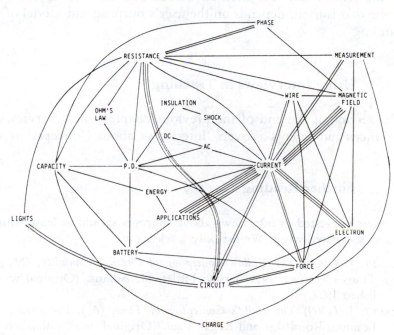

*Figure 5.4:* Maps of associations between concepts from two interview protocols. Upper set from protocol in Figures 5.2 and 5.3

gained only from listening to a recording of the interview or, better still, by being there. It is an impression of the *availability* of the knowledge, the readiness with which the person recalls it. Although not everyone will agree, we accept that a statement that is produced without hesitation and corrections is understood better than one that emerges after false starts and is expressed doubtfully. We would grade more highly the understanding of a person whose responses in an interview were mainly of the former style. Of course, this is subjective and one must beware of differences in personality — a dogmatic and ignorant person might make crisp statements while a cautious and diffident one might appear less comprehending. However, *availability*, a measure of the ease with which knowledge is recalled, is a property of understanding in which a teacher or researcher could be interested. It should be noted that it is a property that is weighted strongly in examinations that have a time limit, as most do.

It is apparent that scoring of interviews can range from a simple summary subjective measure, which may be quite suitable for many purposes of teachers, to specialised vectors of scores on numerous dimensions, that will be tedious to compute and normally of value to researchers rather than teachers. This is an elaborate demonstration of the truism that the method of scoring, as well as the form of probe that is used, depends on the user's purpose and model of understanding.

## Using Interviews in Teaching

The section at the end of the previous chapter, on 'Interviews about Instances and Events', covers 'Interviews about Concepts' as well.

## Further Reading

Anyone interested in interviews about concepts should at least sample Jean Piaget's massive work. We list only a selection:

PIAGET, J. (1969) *The Child's Conception of Physical Causality*, (M. Gabain, Trans.) Totowa, New Jersey: Littlefield, Adams. (Original work published 1927.)

PIAGET, J. (1969) *The Child's Conception of Time*, (A.J. Pomerans, Trans.), London: Routledge and Kegan Paul. (Original work published 1946.)

PIAGET, J. (1970) *The Child's Conception of Movement and Speed*, (G.E.T.

Holloway and M.J. Mackenzie, Trans.), London: Routledge and Kegan Paul. (Original work published 1946.)

A useful compendium of Piaget's work is:

GRUBER, H.E. and VONECHE, J.J. (Eds) (1977) *The Essential Piaget*, London: Routledge and Kegan Paul.

A less readily available, but very useful reference is:

PINES, A.L., NOVAK, J.D., POSNER, G.J. and VAN KIRK, J. (1978) *The Use of Clinical Interviews to Assess Cognitive Structure*, Ithaca, New York: Cornell University Department of Education.

## Chapter 6

# Drawings

In the first day of a year's pre-service course for secondary school teachers, we asked the students to draw a picture of a teacher teaching a class. Figure 6.1 shows some typical examples: the teacher dominates the scene and the students are in orderly rows.

The students repeated the task at the end of the year. The drawings in Figure 6.2 show that their understanding of the work of the teacher has changed: the teacher is a co-worker rather than a controller, the class can work together in small groups, and flexible arrangements are possible.

There is heavy reliance on words in most commonly-used tests of understanding. One of our purposes in this book is to show how probes of understanding can take a wider variety of form. The balance between words and diagrams shifts between the techniques of concept maps, fortune lines and relational diagrams and so on. Here in drawings we have the extreme shift of the balance: practically no words at all, other than those in the instructions and any that the students choose to put into their drawings.

The word-diagram dimension is not the only dimension on which drawings lie towards an extreme. Probes vary in the degree to which they limit students' responses: multiple-choice tests are at an extreme of limitation, short answer questions are a little more open, essays even more so; relational diagrams and fortune lines are more limiting than concept maps. Drawings are very open, with few limits on how the student may respond. Closed and open methods are both valuable, and we need to appreciate that both sorts exist and that they may tap different aspects of understanding.

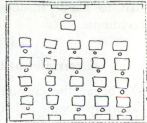

Figure 6.1: *Drawings of 'a teacher teaching a class' made by students at the beginning of a course in teacher training*

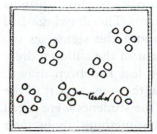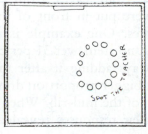

Figure 6.2: *Drawings of 'a teacher teaching a class' made by students at the end of a course in teacher training*

## Purposes of Drawings

The purpose of drawings as a probe of understanding flows from their extreme positions on the word–diagram and closed–open dimensions. They allow the teacher to see, and the student to reveal, qualities of understanding that are hidden from other procedures. It is consistent with the nature of the technique that it is easier for us to show some of those qualities through examples than through writing about them.

## Procedure

We have found that the simple instruction, 'Draw a . . .' works well with students of all ages. Sometimes we have given the students the materials for the drawing, sometimes we have relied on whatever they had to hand. It does not seem to matter, since this is a robust technique.

## Examples of Drawings

We began the chapter with examples of drawings of teachers. The drawings people did at the start of their year of pre-service training as teachers showed that stereotypic, old-fashioned understandings of the teacher's role were common. Stereotypes may be regrettable, but they are part of people's understanding. They can even affect representations people have for objects in plain sight, as Symington, Boundy, Radford and Walton (1981) found when they asked 432 children of ages from 5 to 8 to draw four leaves, from an oak, an elm, a prunus and a eucalypt, that were put in front of them. The drawings had many interesting features. One example is about the stems on the leaves. The elm leaf had no stem, yet 31 per cent of the children drew it with one, nearly always adding it after the leaf had been drawn, whereas with the oak a bigger proportion drew the stem as part of the edge or as an extension of the mid-rib. When the students were asked about the elm stem, their responses revealed something about their understanding of leaves:

> *Observer*   (pointing to drawing of elm):   You put a stem on it.
> *Student*:   Yes.
> *Observer*:   Why?
> *Student*:   It's better with a stem.
> *Observer*:   Why is it better with a stem?
> *Student*:   They can't go on a tree without a stem.
> (Symington, Boundy, Radford and Walton, 1981, p. 48)

Drawings by primary school students of scientists reveal even more stereotyped understandings. Chambers (1983) collected 4807 drawings of scientists from children in the United States, Canada and Australia. Only 28 of them showed a women scientist, all drawn by girls. The drawings conformed closely to the image of scientists that Mead and Metraux (1957) found to be standard among secondary school students in the United States:

> *The scientist is a man who wears a white coat and works in a laboratory. He is elderly or middle aged and wears glasses. He is small, sometimes small and stout, or tall and thin. He may be bald. He may wear a beard, may be unshaven and unkempt. He may be stooped and tired.*

Figure 6.3: *Drawings that reveal conceptions of abstract terms*

*He is surrounded by equipment: test tubes, bunsen burners, flasks and bottles, a jungle gym of blown glass tubes and weird machines with dials. The sparkling white laboratory is full of sounds: the bubbling of liquids in test tubes and flasks, the squeaks and squeals of laboratory animals, the muttering voice of the scientist.*

*He spends his days doing experiments. He pours chemicals from one test tube into another. He peers raptly through microscopes. He scans the heavens through a telescope [or a microscope!] He experiments with plants and animals, cutting them apart, injecting serum into animals. He writes neatly in black notebooks.* (Mead and Metraux, 1957, pp. 386–7, italics in original)

The drawings of scientists show a particular understanding of science. Interviews could also uncover that understanding, but drawings reveal it efficiently and effectively, and perhaps with a directness that is more compelling than is possible through words.

The drawings of teachers and scientists bring out an affective component of understanding that most other probes leave untapped. The drawer's feelings about the subject may appear, as the examples in Figure 6.3 show. We collected the examples from people of a wide range of ages and interests.

### Introducing Drawings to Students

We have not had any trouble in getting people to draw things, not even abstract ideas like justice. Sometimes we have to assure them that we are not looking for high artistic or draughting performance, but soon all are at work. People like to draw. We have not even had to provide examples, which is as well since examples could influence the response.

Adults appear a little more inhibited than children in drawing, more likely to say that they have never been able to draw. They may need more encouragement. Young students may need more help with abstractions. Where adults are ready to draw 'kindness', children may have to be asked to draw 'someone being kind'.

### Variations and Extensions

At first we used drawings with real things, such as teachers, which are visible or even present, then tried them with invisible objects such as micro-organisms, and later found them useful with abstractions such as kindness. In all cases we have found that drawings provide insights into understanding that are often surprising. We have not tried them with historical or contemporary figures (Julius Caesar, Saddam Husein) or with real or fictional incidents, but we believe that these applications, too, would be revealing.

As well as varying the type of subject for drawings you can change the procedure. One useful extension is to ask students for a series of drawings of a changing situation. Novick and Nussbaum (1978) were interested in 13- and 14-year-old students' understandings of what they had been taught a year earlier about gases. The students were supposed to understand that gases are composed of invisible particles that move ceaselessly, scattered more or less evenly in any enclosed space, with empty spaces between them. Together with oral interviews, Novick and Nussbaum showed the students a flask and a vacuum pump and asked them 'If you were able to see the air in the flask, draw how it would look before and after the vacuum pump was used to remove some of the air'. Examples of some of the drawings are shown in Figure 6.4.

The drawings A and B illustrate one problem with drawings: they have to be interpreted by the prober, who may infer incorrectly the meaning that the drawer meant to represent. Thus it is not certain that those drawings show a belief that gases are continuous rather than

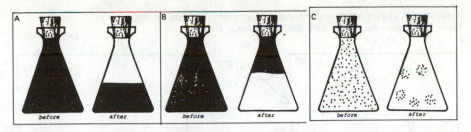

Figure 6.4:  *Students' drawings of gases before and after some gas was withdrawn from a flask (from Novick and Nussbaum, 1978)*

particulate; for their drawers might have meant to indicate that the particles are so small and numerous that if the gas became visible it would *look* continuous, as coloured gases in fact do. Problems with interpretation are not peculiar to drawings, of course. In all probes the precision and sensitivity of the assessment are increased greatly when they can be supplemented with an interview, to ask why the respondent drew or wrote something in a particular way, and that is certainly true of drawings.

A variation of the sequential drawings procedure is to provide students with a drawing and ask them to draw what it would look like after some change. This is a more controlled use of drawing as a probe of understanding, but can still yield surprising and revealing responses. One of us had taught year 8 students about photosynthesis, and had said that 'green plants make their own food from carbon dioxide and water, using light energy'; also that 'green plants grow towards the light', and that 'mushrooms are not green plants, so do not make their own food'. To test understanding of this, the students were given a drawing of a green plant and a mushroom in a box, with light coming in from the side. They had to draw what it would look like in a week's time, with the expectation that they would show the green plant bending towards the light. Lila's response (Figure 6.5) showed an unexpected interpretation.

The ambiguous object protruding under the cap of the mushroom is a leaf. Lila said, 'The mushroom couldn't make its own food, so it ate the green plant'. That suggests another extension, of asking students to write explanations of their diagrams.

## What the Procedure Reveals

Drawings are the most open-ended of techniques, so can reveal unsuspected understandings. The more closed the technique, the more the

The diagram shows a green plant and a mushroom in a box. In the blank box draw what it will look like in a week's time.

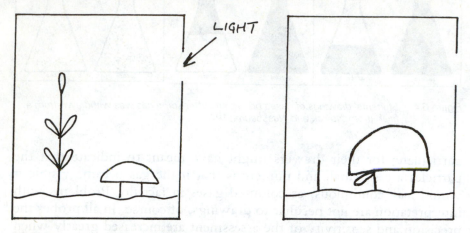

LIGHT

*Figure 6.5:    Student's drawing (on right) revealing unsuspected interpretation of statement that 'mushrooms cannot make their own food'*

respondents are confined to matching parts of their understandings to that of the prober, and the more hidden remain the other parts. Drawings, however, may reveal those hidden, unsuspected parts. It is hard to imagine how Symington and his co-workers could have discovered in any other way the extent to which children's observations and images of leaves are affected by stereotypes. Novick and Nussbaum could have asked for verbal descriptions of the distribution of gas molecules in a flask, but that would have been less efficient and the responses may have been less easy to interpret.

Drawings tap holistic understanding. They allow expression of attitudes or feelings as well as cognition. The drawings of teachers (Figures 6.1 and 6.2) and of abstractions (Figure 6.3) show this.

### Scoring of Drawings

Our reservations about reducing so complex a property as understanding to a number apply as strongly to drawings as to any technique. Drawings reveal *types* of understanding rather than points on a uni-dimensional continuum. The drawings of teachers (Figures 6.1 and 6.2) show this. You could score these drawings for amount of change in desired direction from before the training course to after, though it would be subjective. Leaf drawings could be scored for resemblance to the model leaves. The gas molecule drawings of

Novick and Nussbaum could be scored correct or incorrect. But in every case reducing the rich data of the drawing to a score destroys information.

It may be that, even though you appreciate that a score represents only a fraction of the information in a drawing, for some purpose you still want to arrive at a summary number. It is impossible to give rules for doing this, since drawings can be used to test understanding of an enormous range of ideas and for a range of purposes. Rules for scoring leaf drawings are unlikely to apply to rules for scoring drawings of teachers, or of kindness. It is even difficult in most applications to lay down beforehand criteria for good understanding that a drawing should show. The openness of the technique is coupled with a difficulty in establishing reliable procedures for scoring.

## Using Drawings in Teaching

Drawings reveal to teacher *and* student the ideas held by the student. The responses to the draw-a-teacher task shown in Figures 6.1 and 6.2 are an instance. There was a deliberate teaching purpose in calling for them. The first set of drawings was made on the first day of a year-long pre-service teacher education course; they revealed to the students themselves some of their beliefs and attitudes about teaching. The second set, from the end of the course, had the purpose not only of again revealing to the students their current beliefs but also of enabling them to reflect on shifts that had occurred in their views through the year.

Other procedures such as essays or attitude measures can also document shifts in views, but drawings are an efficient and effective method: efficient, in that they contain much information in a single sheet that takes little time to complete; and effective in that they are easily assimilated by the person looking at them, especially when the viewer is the drawer. We find that few people fail to appreciate the significance of changes apparent in their drawings.

Learning involves change in ideas and beliefs, of course, but often the change is imperceptible to the learner. Awareness of change is important, since it is a first step to gaining greater control of learning — that is, towards becoming a better learner. Most people find drawings fun to do, which is good, but what is even better is that drawings enable teachers to discuss learning and students to reflect on their own learning, both of factual content and of attitudes. Thus drawings are a useful means of improving learning styles.

### Further Reading

The example of drawing a teacher, which began this chapter, goes back at least thirty years. Travers and Rabinowitz used it as a projective measure of teacher personality, though we see it as a measure of perception of the relation between teacher's and students' roles.

TRAVERS, R.M.W. and RABINOWITZ, W. (1953) 'A drawing technique for studying certain outcomes of teacher education, Part II. A quantitative comparison of certain outcomes in two institutions'. R.M.W. TRAVERS, W. RABINOWITZ, M.H. PAGE, E. NAMOVICHER and P. VENTUR, *Exploratory Studies in Teacher Personality*, New York: City Colleges, Division of Teacher Education.

Mead and Metraux, and Chambers, used drawings to probe images of scientists:

MEAD, M. and METRAUX, R. (1957) 'The image of the scientist among high school students: A pilot study', *Science*, **126**, pp. 384–90.
CHAMBERS, D.W. (1983) 'Stereotypic images of the scientist: The draw-a-scientist test', *Science Education*, **67**, pp. 255–65.

The draw-a-teacher or scientist tasks reveal images, which we consider part of understanding. The only published examples we have of drawings used to probe understandings of non-human objects or concepts are the studies by Novick and Nussbaum, and Symington *et al.*

NOVICK, S. and NUSSBAUM, J. (1978) 'Junior high school pupils' understanding of the particulate nature of matter: An interview study', *Science Education*, **62**, pp. 273–81.
SYMINGTON, D., BOUNDY, K., RADFORD, T. and WALTON, J. (1981) 'Children's drawings of natural phenomena', *Research in Science Education*, **11**, pp. 44–51.

*Chapter 7*

# Fortune Lines

Novels, plays, epic poems, music, and history all present a story that unfolds as a sequence of scenes. Fortune lines probe learners' understanding of the story by requiring them to estimate and graph one or more quantities for each scene.

The technique was invented by Laurence Rush (1988), who provides as an example the story of Little Red Riding Hood. This nursery story can be separated into ten scenes:

> Little Red Riding Hood sets off from home
> Little Red Riding Hood enters wood
> Little Red Riding Hood meets wolf
> Little Red Riding Hood escapes from wolf, continues through wood
> Little Red Riding Hood comes to grandma's cottage
> 'What big eyes you have'
> 'What big ears you have'
> 'What big teeth you have' — wolf unmasks, pursues
> Hunter enters, kills wolf
> Grandma found unhurt in cupboard

One dimension that changes through the story is Little Red Riding Hood's peace of mind, or happiness. A child who understands the story might graph that dimension as shown in Figure 7.1.

For a child who understands the technique of graphing, any major variation from the form shown in Figure 7.1 would indicate a difference in understanding from that accepted by the teacher.

## Purpose of Fortune Lines

Long-established ways of testing understanding of extended communications such as novels or chapters of history are to ask students

107

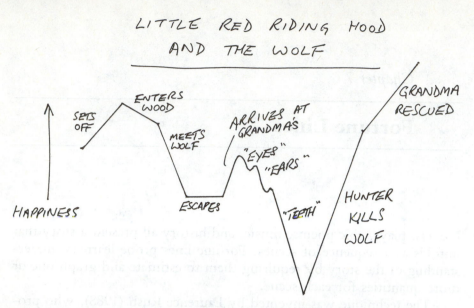

*Figure 7.1: Fortune line for 'Little Red Riding Hood'*

to write essays about them ('Describe the events from the Austrian Anschluss leading up to the outbreak of the Second World War'), to write a paragraph about a limited point ('Discuss the options open to the British government in response to the German demands on the Sudetenland in 1938'), and to answer specific questions ('Who were the signatories of the Munich "piece of paper"?'). All three procedures reveal aspects of understanding that fortune lines cannot tap; the function of fortune lines is to supplement, not replace, these traditional techniques.

Fortune lines do have properties that make that supplementation valuable. Assessment of understanding through essays and paragraphs is confounded by wide variations in students' skills of writing. On the one hand a student with poor skills will find it difficult to express clearly what might be an adequate or even superior understanding, while on the other a fluent writer might get away with disguising shallow perception in a flow of words — especially when the marker is tired or numbed by a long succession of essays beforehand. By requiring a response in a different, non-verbal form, the fortune line method overcomes that confounding. Of course there can be wide variations in graphing ability, too, but it is a simpler skill than essay writing and also provides a different opportunity for expression.

It is also easier to express gradations of quantities such as happiness, interest, power, or kindness by a graph than by words. The relative heights of peaks of Red Riding Hood's happiness would be difficult or tedious to express in words, but can be shown economically with a simple graph. Fortune lines are also economical in the time they take to assess.

In sum, the purpose of fortune lines is to supplement traditional forms of assessment of understanding for extended communications that present a sequence of scenes.

## Procedure

No special materials are needed. At some time after the students have read the communication, the teacher lists its events in the order in which they occurred.

An example for Dickens' novel *Oliver Twist* could be:

1  Oliver grows up in the parish workhouse.
2  Oliver asks for more.
3  Oliver is sold to the Sowerberrys.
4  Oliver runs away.
5  Fagin takes in Oliver.
6  Oliver is accused of stealing Mr Brownlow's handkerchief.
7  Oliver is succoured by Mr Brownlow and Mrs Bedwin.
8  Fagin's gang recaptures Oliver.
9  Bill Sikes takes Oliver to burgle a house, where he is wounded.
10  Mrs Maylie and Rose look after Oliver.
11  Nancy is murdered, Sikes killed, and the gang captured.
12  Rose is discovered to be Oliver's aunt, and Mr Brownlow adopts Oliver.

The students may have individual copies of the list, or the teacher can put it on the board. The teacher tells the students to sketch a graph of Oliver's fortune through the twelve successive scenes.

Useful instructions to students are:

1  Make a rough draft first
   — use the full width of the page
   — use a line for each event (16 events = 16 joined lines)
   — improving fortune
   — worsening fortune
   — no change
   — fluctuating fortune

2  Heighten peaks to represent highest fortunes;
   deepen troughs to represent lowest fortunes
3  Make a neat final copy
   — include a title
   — put the number of each event at the mid–point of its
     line                                    (Rush, 1988, pp. 26–7)

The students can be set to do the task in class or for homework.


## Examples of Fortune Lines

Since fortune lines are a new invention we have not had much experience with them. Our examples are, therefore, mostly suggestions rather than well-tried instances.

Music should be a suitable subject for use of fortune lines. Plots of operas could be sub-divided into scenes, and graded on appropriate dimensions. Mozart's *Don Giovanni* would provide rich possibilities — lines for Donna Elvira's attraction to the Don, for Masetto's happiness, for Leporello's contentment in his service, and even for the spectator's own emotional reactions such as respect for Don Giovanni (which for most should rise at the end when he meets the statue and death with courage). Musical scores could also be divided into sections, and lines drawn for characteristics such as richness of colour, complexity of scoring, or emotional reactions.

Fortune lines can reveal understanding of historical events. The Battle of the Atlantic in World War 2, for instance, can be represented in a manageable number of phases: the early days beginning with the sinking of the *Athenia* to the organization of convoys, German capture of French Atlantic ports, sinking of the Graf Spee, lease of 50 US destroyers to Britain, destruction of the French fleet at Oran, sinking of the Bismarck, development of wolf-pack tactics, entry of the United States into the war, introduction of the snorkel and of radar, the Allied invasion of France. Graphs could be called for of the balance of fortune of the Allied and Axis powers.

A similar use is possible with contemporary social events: the popularity of the government, the probability of the continuation of human life, the level of tolerance in a community. Each of these dimensions can be mapped against a series of events. Nor need events be contemporary, social or even to do with humans at all: the events could be geological, and the dimension the diversity of living species.

We can, through Rush (1988), provide one example in detail. It is for the early Australian novel, *For the Term of His Natural Life*, in which the protagonist, Rufus Dawes, is unjustly convicted and transported to the convict colony. Rush divided the second half of the novel into sixteen scenes:

*The continuing fortunes of Rufus Dawes*
1  Discovers that Sylvia is alive
2  Escapes and talks to Sylvia
3  Sylvia is afraid of him and screams for help
4  Refuses to continue to flog Kirkland
5  Gets 100 lashes for disobedience
6  Leads the Norfolk Island 'Ring' and terrorizes the guards
7  Frere is appointed Commandant and picks on Dawes
8  Gets Sylvia's rosebud from Rev. North
9  Makes a murder pact and draws straws
10  Put on 'stretcher' by Frere
11  Released by Sylvia
12  Discovers that North is in love with Sylvia
13  Tells North his full life story
14  Escapes from prison
15  Meets Sylvia as ship sinks and she regains her memory
16  Both drown

Rush's own graph of Dawes' fortune is shown in Figure 7.2. In the section on scoring we compare this line with those produced by some of his students.

## Introducing Fortune Lines to Students

The fortune line is a sophisticated technique that students take time to learn. Before you give them one to do on their own it is sensible to work through one with the whole class, using a simple story that is well-known to all like Little Red Riding Hood. The representation of increasing and decreasing happiness by the slope of a line can be explained by example.

Immediately following the class teaching, the students should attempt a line for a very simple story such as a nursery rhyme, for which there are only two or three scenes. For example, the happiness of the dog in

(*Scene 1*)  Old Mother Hubbard went to the cupboard
            To fetch the poor dog a bone

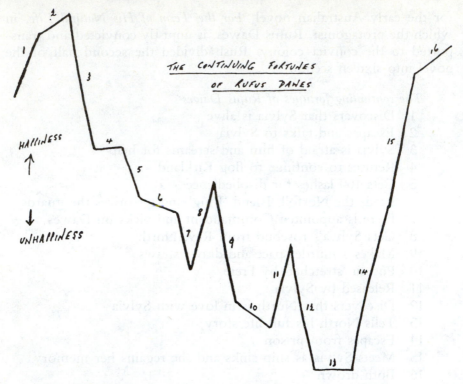

Figure 7.2:   *Teacher's line for the fortunes of Rufus Dawes*

(*Scene 2*)   But when she got there the cupboard was bare
And so the poor dog had none.

Presumably most would draw a rising followed by a falling line. If they all do, it might be possible to draw students' attention to relative heights and depths by asking them to consider the alternatives in Figure 7.3, and to discuss these with them.

The students should have further practice with simple stories or with events that they themselves had experienced recently. The teacher should provide them with clear descriptions of the scenes in the stories or events, since sorting out the events is an advanced skill.

The first application to an extended story, such as *For the Term of His Natural Life*, should be to an unambiguous story with clear-cut scenes. Later applications can be to complex plots. Discussion should follow any use of fortune lines, but is particularly useful following the first attempt.

It might be wise to leave the advanced techniques of curved lines

Which of these lines is best to show the feelings of the dog in
'Old Mother Hubbard'?

*Figure 7.3: Fortune lines used to stimulate discussion*

to represent fluctuating fortune within a scene and of requiring students to select their own scenes until they are familiar with the basic
method. The time that that will take will of course depend on the
sophistication of the students, but as a rough rule we suggest that they
should have done at least four basic lines first. Most students will soon
comprehend the notion of using sloping lines to represent increasing
and decreasing fortunes (or other qualities), but it takes longer for
them to appreciate the subtleties of relative heights and depths. Consider Anthea's line in Figure 7.5, in the section on 'What the Procedure
Reveals': all the lines have the same magnitude of slope, so that the
peak is simply the cumulation of a number of positive scenes and the
trough of negatives; there is no notion of a sudden, appalling drop in
happiness such as most comprehending readers would see in Scene 3
or the soaring in delight that Dawes experiences in Scene 15 when
Sylvia regains her memory. Anthea understands the story well, but
has more to learn about representing her understanding in a fortune
line.

Fortune lines can be used effectively without ever extending to
student selection of scenes. However, that extension is powerful. If it
is attempted, the teacher must appreciate that students need training
and practice in selecting scenes. At first they find it difficult to sort out
events, and tend to pick out a few key incidents when the nature of
fortune lines requires sequential, linked scenes. Training might begin
by a class lesson in which students are asked to identify the first scene
for a story. The class could discuss their opinions, and then adopt a con-
sensus answer. Then the second scene could be identified, and so on.

## Variations and Extensions

The graph in the example of *For the Term of His Natural Life* charts a reader's estimate of Rufus Dawes' perception of his fortune, or his happiness. Fortune lines can be applied to many other dimensions, including qualities that the principal character does not necessarily perceive, such as sanity, alertness, and nobility. Thus a fortune line could represent the viciousness of Heathcliff's actions in *Wuthering Heights* or the moral greatness of Sydney Carton in *A Tale of Two Cities*. These instances are, oddly, more subjective than judgements of a character's perceptions of his or her own fortune, since they depend so much on the student's beliefs about viciousness and morality, more personal and debatable concepts than happiness or fortune. Still, subjectivity is an element that should not be ruled out of understanding; merely because someone has a different opinion about morality than you does not mean that their understanding is deficient.

The dimension in a fortune line can apply to a nation or an organization as well as to an individual. An example could be the polarisation of opinion about Vietnam in the United States across a sequence of events from the increased provision of military advisers in 1960 through the Tonkin Gulf incident, the bombing of North Vietnam, the landing of marines at Da Nang in 1965, the build-up of US forces, the Tet Offensive in 1968, the cessation of bombing of the North, Johnson's refusal to stand for re-election, the invasion of Kampuchea, the withdrawal of US forces in 1973, and the fall of Saigon in 1975.

The dimension can also be a condition of the students themselves, such as interest in the story, sympathy for a given character, or how funny or exciting they found it.

A powerful extension of the fortune line technique is to require students to graph together two or more dimensions, which could be different quantities for one character or perceptions of the one quantity by different characters. Thus graphs might be drawn for Tom Sawyer's enjoyment during various scenes and of his responsibility, plus the peace of mind of his Aunt Polly at the same time.

A different style of extension is to use fortune lines to reveal feelings about actual experiences. We have done this with university graduates who were doing a year of pre-service training to become teachers. The year involves them in periods at the university, when they attend courses in teaching method, learning theory, and history and sociology of education, and periods in schools known as teaching rounds, when they teach under the guidance of supervisors. It is a

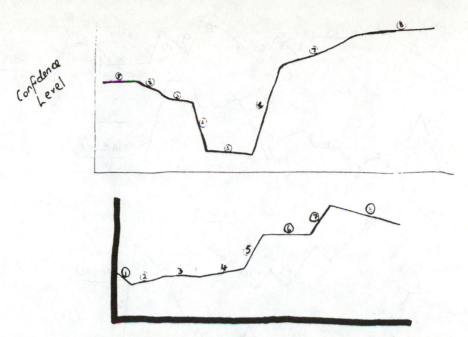

*Figure 7.4: Fortune lines drawn by two students to represent their self-confidence through periods in their pre-service year of teacher training*

year of coping with new experiences. Figure 7.4 shows fortune lines that students drew for their self-confidence through eight periods from the beginning to the middle of the year. The eight periods are:

1 The week before the course began
2 The first few days of the course, at university
3 The five weeks at university before the first teaching round
4 The first teaching round, three weeks
5 Vacation of two weeks
6 Three weeks at the university
7 The second teaching round
8 Four weeks at the university

Although this application is more to feelings than to knowledge, we see it as probing an aspect of understanding. The lines told us much about individuals' progress and about the general effect of the various segments of the course.

## What the Procedure Reveals

Fortune lines provide rapid insights into the quality of students' understanding of individual scenes and of their place in the complete

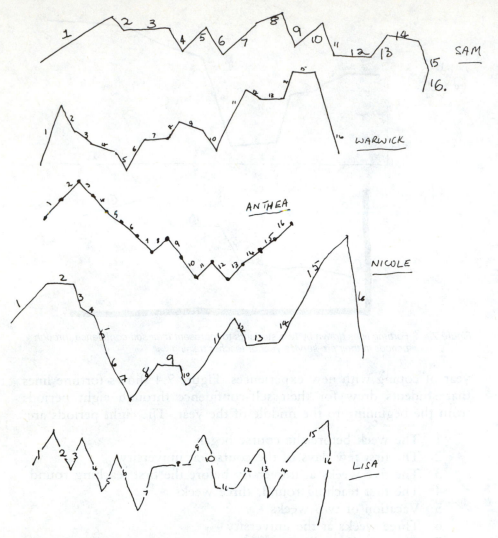

Figure 7.5: Students' lines for the fortunes of Rufus Dawes

story. Rush's grade 9 students drew the examples in Figure 7.5 for the sixteen scenes from *For the Term of His Natural Life* described in the 'Examples' section. From the figure it is simple to see that Warwick, Anthea and Nicole have reasonable understandings of *For the Term of His Natural Life*, while Sam and Lisa do not. A little further inspection shows that Anthea has a very sound comprehension, Nicole has the story well in hand though needs to be asked about her perception of Scene 9, and Warwick seems to be off track with a small number of scenes.

116

The lines reveal basic misunderstandings. In Scene 5, for instance, Dawes receives a brutal and unjust flogging, yet Sam and Lisa rate his fortune as improving. Sam's whole response indicates little appreciation of what happens in the novel, or perhaps inability to convert his appreciation to a sensible line. He rates Dawes' fortune as improving when his enemy, the vicious Frere, is put in power over him, and when he is racked in Scene 10. The line shows that Sam is having trouble.

Warwick's line reveals a better understanding, but even he rates Scene 7, Frere's appointment, as neutral in its effect on Dawes' fortune, where most readers who appreciate the relation between the two men read this scene with foreboding for Dawes. Perhaps Warwick saw the appointment itself as neutral, waiting for its consequences before judging that Dawes' fortune had declined. As with most pencil-and-paper tests, one would want to follow up with an interview to sort out issues like that.

Not all scenes are as clear-cut as the flogging and racking ones; Scene 12 is complex in that Dawes knows that North is well-meaning towards him, but Dawes loves Sylvia too even though he has no prospects of requiting that love; then, too, Sylvia is married. The complexity of issues makes it difficult to judge whether the discovery of North's love for Sylvia improves or worsens Dawes' fortune. The students who overall reveal superior understanding, Warwick, Anthea, and Nicole, all rate the scene as a moderate decline for Dawes, an assessment with which most adults familiar with the novel might agree. Sam and Lisa have different views.

The final scene is even more difficult. A mature appreciation might see that the deaths of Dawes and Sylvia are positive, with both escaping at last from intolerable experiences. A parallel is the apotheosis of the Dutchman and Senta at the end of Wagner's opera *Der Fliegende Holländer*. Though Sam, Warwick, Nicole, and Lisa follow more conventional views in rating death as the ultimate misfortune, Anthea continues with an upwards line. Whether she really saw that Dawes and Sylvia had escaped from misery, rejection, injustice and hate is not certain, though her assessments of the earlier scenes give an impression that she understands what is happening. An interview would help to sort this out.

Sometimes, either because of the way they interpret a scene or because of some flaw in the teaching, a whole class will draw a segment in the direction opposite to the way the teacher expected. Such an occurrence is readily apparent, and alerts the teacher to the need to take action.

For assessing the understanding both of individuals and the whole class, fortune lines are sharper probes than another technique that can be used with stories, concept maps. There is more precision in fortune lines, a much clearer notion of right and wrong. It is harder to disguise lack of understanding in a fortune line. A more subtle point is that the relations that students tend to represent in concept maps are factual and static, where in fortune lines the relations that matter are conceptual and fluctuating. Thus where a fortune line could be used to probe understanding of the development of the Reverend North's sympathy for Dawes, a concept map would represent that relation, if the student chose to include it at all, by a single statement such as 'sympathises with'. Concept maps do have the advantage of being applicable to any sort of relation between terms, where fortune lines can be used only where there is a succession of scenes. Further, fortune lines concentrate on the understanding of the development of one quality, or a very small number of qualities, while concept maps range over the whole spectrum of relations. This comparison exemplifies a general principle, that the more specialised the probe the sharper its bite, and the more precise the assessment it will provide of the student's understanding. Fortune lines are a sharper probe than concept maps.

The more the students get used to fortune lines, the better the lines will reveal understanding. The relative heights and depths, the corresponding slopes of lines, and the introduction of curved segments will all show shades of meaning that are difficult to put into words but are easy to graph. Essays, though, should not be abandoned since students need to learn how to put subtle ideas into words; it is just that fortune lines are a powerful supplement to essays.

One shortcoming of fortune lines is that the reasons behind a student's choices for slopes are not apparent. The line needs to be followed with an interview or with a requirement for the student to write a justification for each segment. The latter extension is a useful synthesis of fortune line with essay; where essays can be rambling, tying one to a fortune line provides structure. The reasons the student gives for each segment constitute a deep probe of understanding.

An advantage of fortune lines over essays is that they are not laborious to do. Once the thinking part has been done, it is easy to draw the line. A consequence of this is that students are more ready to consider new information and other points of view, and to change their lines; whereas essays, once done, are finished with. Similarly, students are rarely willing to write a second or third essay about a topic, but will re-do fortune lines. This means that a teacher may probe understanding of a story several times, say after first reading, after class lessons and discussion, and much later after the students have read and reflected upon other books. Fortune lines are useful in following the development of understanding.

Constructing a fortune line requires students to consider knowledge from outside each scene, either from within the story from other scenes or from outside the story altogether. The rating of Scene 6 in *For the Term of His Natural Life*, for instance, in which Dawes leads the convicts in terrorizing the guards, requires understanding of the conditions on Norfolk Island, which the book makes clear, and also of the power of government and bureaucracies, which students may have learned from their own lives. Without the latter understanding, students may see the scene as an increase in Dawes' fortune where more experienced readers know that in it things are turning worse for him. Fortune lines, therefore, allow assessment of the student's understanding of the story *in context*, a useful property.

## Scoring of Fortune Lines

Analysis of fortune lines will reveal problems that a class may have had with particular scenes, and will show which students have failed to understand. The analysis depends on the teacher determining his or her own prepared line and comparing each segment of it with the students'. The comparison can be reported to the students, with or without an overall assessment and score. Rush recommends marking each segment with × = wrong slope, √ = correct slope, or ? = please explain. The provision of the *please explain* mark is sensible, since it allows for clearer probing of matters such as Anthea's rating of segment 16. Assessments for the examples of Figure 7.5 are shown in Figure 7.6.

If required, the lines or the assessments of Figure 7.6 can be converted to a summary number. This can be done either by a subjective judgement (Warwick B+, Sam E) or by a simple rule such as score 1 for each correct segment (Warwick 12, Sam 6). However, as with all of the probes described in this book, the real value of fortune lines is not in the summary score but in the insight provided into the quality of the students' understandings and the sharpness with which one can identify specific misunderstandings of both the whole class and of individuals.

| | Scene | | | | | | | | | | | | | | | |
|---|---|---|---|---|---|---|---|---|---|---|---|---|---|---|---|---|
| | 1 | 2 | 3 | 4 | 5 | 6 | 7 | 8 | 9 | 10 | 11 | 12 | 13 | 14 | 15 | 16 |
| Acceptable response | ↗ | ↗ | ↘ | ↗→ | ↘ | ↘ | ↘ | ↗ | ↘ | ↘ | ↗ | ↘ | →↗ | ↗ | ↗ | ↘ |
| Anthea | ✓ | ✓ | ✓ | ✓ | ✓ | ✓ | ✓ | ✓ | ✓ | ✓ | ✓ | ✓ | ✓ | ✓ | ✓ | ? |
| Nicole | ✓ | ? | ✓ | ✓ | ✓ | ✓ | ✓ | ✓ | X | ✓ | ✓ | ✓ | ✓ | ✓ | ✓ | ? |
| Warwick | ✓ | X | ✓ | ✓ | ✓ | X | X | ✓ | ✓ | ✓ | ✓ | ✓ | ✓ | ✓ | X | ? |
| Lisa | ✓ | X | X | ? | X | ✓ | X | X | X | ✓ | X | X | X | ✓ | ✓ | ? |
| Sam | ✓ | X | X | X | X | ✓ | X | ✓ | ✓ | X | X | X | ✓ | X | X | ? |

*Figure 7.6:   Analysis of fortune lines from Figure 7.5*

## Using Fortune Lines in Teaching

One of the advantages of fortune lines is that they allow the teacher to focus the students' attention on an aspect of a story, which exhortation often fails to do. They are a means, for instance, of teaching students how to assess the development of the plot or the relations between characters. Through doing fortune lines students learn how to think about each scene and its function within the story. Relative heights and depths cause them to consider the balance of a story. These things are not easy to teach by other means.

Students learn from fortune lines to link events, and to analyse what is changing in each scene. They learn to consider the effect one character has on another, and to read the story from the points of view of the characters. This is one way in which they can learn tolerance of other people's views, learning which is further encouraged by discussion of different fortune lines and the rating of debatable scenes such as the deaths of Dawes and Sylvia.

Fortune lines are readily discussed, and allow students to build their understandings of the story as they and their classmates justify their decisions about each scene and as they consider whether to change those decisions. Discussion need not be limited to post mortems of individuals' lines: constructing a line can be a group activity that will promote discussion within and between groups as the lines are being formed.

Even when a fortune line is not the required outcome, students may find them helpful in tasks such as writing an essay or a story. An exercise such as 'Describe the relations between Napoleon and the Directory' may be easier if the form of the essay is determined by first sketching a few fortune lines for dimensions such as Napoleon's dependence on Barras, popular support for the Directory, and France's military fortunes. In the same way, lines can be used in planning the teaching of a story. When the teacher has drawn a few lines for the story, it will be easy to keep the lesson on track.

### Summary Points

Rush (1988) lists advantages and disadvantages of fortune lines, and makes recommendations for their use.

*Advantages:*

— It forces students to recall events
— It focusses attention on key events
— It forces students to make linking relationships
— It provides a structure on which to build understanding
— It forces the making of value judgements
— It has strong visual appeal
— It presents a large amount of information compactly
— It decreases the emphasis on written expression
— It adds variety to lesson format
— Its basic concept is relatively simple
— The line construction itself only takes about ten minutes
— It has a high level of student acceptance
— It provides an excellent basis for follow-up discussion
— It encourages students to take an overall view of events
— It encourages individuality
— It is suitable for small group work
— It highlights weaknesses in understanding key points
— Students can be given responsibility in item selection
— Teachers can control the item selection
— It is very useful as a revision tool.

*Disadvantages:*

— It only suits development which takes place over time
— It needs initial practice with the technique itself
— Assessment is individual and takes a great deal of time

— Paucity of written comment can pose an assessment problem
— Assessment has to consider both slope and written comment
— Additional questioning is often needed for clarification
— Teacher-selection of items gives an inbuilt bias
— The single-line graph may be too simplistic on some occasions, particularly where there are differing short-term and long-term effects.

*Recommendations for the Classroom Use of Fortune Lines:*

— Use it as an aid to enrich a topic
— Practise the technique with the class
— Rough out your own version first
— Use between 6 and 12 items for a fortune line
— A rough draft should be done before the final copy
— Do not attempt student-chosen items until the technique is mastered with teacher-chosen items
— Do not use below Year 8 level
— Keep it to a half-hour or less time span
— If it is taking longer, let it be finished as homework
— If a student is struggling, suggest a joint submission with another student
— Do not overdo the technique — 5 or 6 a year is ample
— Work out your own assessment procedures
— Always allow time for individual or class discussion
— Put selected final copies on display
— Use as a diagram/memory aid during revision sessions
— Try reversing the procedure: give the fortune line first and ask the students to list the events
— Fortune lines for two characters can be put on the same page for comparison

## Further Reading

RUSH, L.N. (1988) *Fortune Lines: A New Probe of Understanding in the Humanities*, Unpublished Master of Educational Studies project, Monash University, Melbourne.

Rush describes his invention of fortune lines, and his experiences in using them in English teaching.

*Chapter 8*

# Relational Diagrams

In a relational diagram a person draws closed figures to show the pattern of overlap between classes of objects, events, or abstractions. Figure 8.1 is an example produced by a 14-year-old student in an Australian social studies class. It demonstrates an accurate knowledge of the relations between the classes.

## Purposes of Relational Diagrams

Nouns are labels given to classes of things. One way of probing understanding of the label is to ask the person to define it. You would often then want to check whether the person understood the terms in the definition. An alternative is to see what sorts of things the person would include under the label, and what exclude. You could test that by asking the person to sort objects into instances and non-instances of the label. Something of that sort is done in interviews about instances (Chapter 4), where the procedure goes on to ask the person why the object is or is not a member of the class. A third way is to see how the person discriminates between the label and related terms, which is the essence of a relational diagram. Its purpose is to probe the meaning that a person has for a term by requiring the person to discriminate between it and related terms.

### Procedure

No materials are required other than pen and paper. Oral instructions suffice.

Suppose that the terms that are being probed are *animals*, *dogs*, *cats*, and *pets*. The instructions would go:

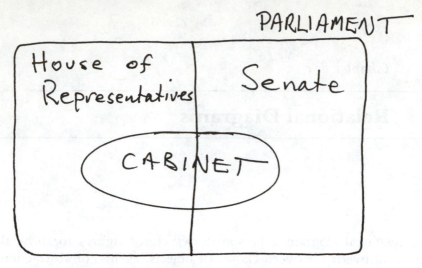

*Figure 8.1: An example of a relational diagram*

1   Draw a large square or circle and label it *animals*.
2   Now draw squares, circles or other shapes on the diagram to represent *dogs*, *cats*, and *pets*, showing how they are related to each other and to *animals*. (The terms should be displayed on the board or screen.)
3   Look carefully at your diagram, think about what it represents, and decide whether you want to change any part of it.

Of course, when students are familiar with the procedure there will hardly be any need to give any instructions at all. One of the merits of the technique is its simplicity.

The shape that students are instructed, or left to choose, to represent a class does not matter — it can be square, circular, oval, or irregular, so long as it is a closed figure.

Both experienced and beginning students should be encouraged to take seriously instruction 3, about checking and changing the diagram. It is important that they perceive that all of the separate areas in the diagram should have some meaning, that none is empty. A routine for checking is to look at each area in the diagram and to ask whether such cases exist. Figure 8.2 illustrates the point.

Part (a) of Figure 8.2 is a diagram drawn by a 10-year-old. The cross has been added by us to pick out an area that discussion with the student discovered to be meaningless. The student did not mean to imply that there were people attending the school who were neither

124

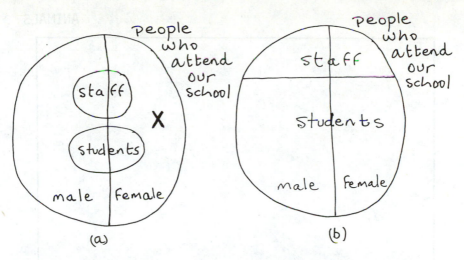

Figure 8.2:   *Relational diagram with an empty, meaningless area (a), and corrected (b)*

staff nor students. Part (b) of the figure is a better representation of the student's understanding of the terms. We have found that some students need considerable experience with relational diagrams before they check their spatial arrangements for empty, meaningless areas. They should be trained in that checking as a standard procedure.

It might be thought that it would be good to require students to make the areas of the shapes correspond to the sizes of the groups they represent. Thus in Figure 8.2 the area for *staff* could have been much smaller than that for *children*. We have found that it is hardly worth the trouble to require this. The added difficulty for students is not compensated for with substantially greater insight into their under-standing. With experienced and able students it can be some use, but otherwise we advise that you reply 'no' if a student asks whether size matters.

Instruction No. 1, which involves providing an over-arching concept, is less necessary for older students or young ones who are experienced in producing relational diagrams. For them, *animal* could have been omitted (although that would have removed the possibility of inferring aspects of understanding about *animal* and *pet*, such as might be shown by students with pet rocks in mind or who have a pet parrot or pet worm that they do not class as an animal). At the other extreme, for younger or inexperienced students, the teacher might prepare a diagram beforehand to represent the over-arching concept, and present it to them on individual sheets of paper or on the board to

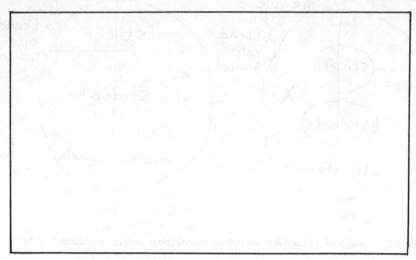

ANIMALS

*Figure 8.3:   A prepared response sheet for a relational diagram task*

copy (Figure 8.3). This will set a pattern for further maps and make the individual productions easier to compare.

## Examples of Relational Diagrams

We chose the examples to illustrate the range of topics in which relational diagrams can be used and the types of responses students make, and to bring out points to consider in using the technique.

The diagrams in Figure 8.4 were produced by (a) a 12-year-old and (b) a university mathematics graduate. The younger student had not yet heard of imaginary or transcendental numbers, for which the graduate has included an area.

Although relational diagrams often refer to classes for which there is authoritative agreement, such as numbers, you can use them for matters in which opinion or taste enters. Figure 8.5 shows how two 17-year-olds in a high school literature class saw the relations between poetry, verse and limericks. Both representations can be defended, and although a teacher might prefer the students to see the relation in one particular way it would be dogmatic to mark one as wrong. Right, wrong, or defensible, each diagram shows clearly how its drawer perceives the relation between the three terms.

We have used the terms in Figure 8.6 quite often as an illustrative

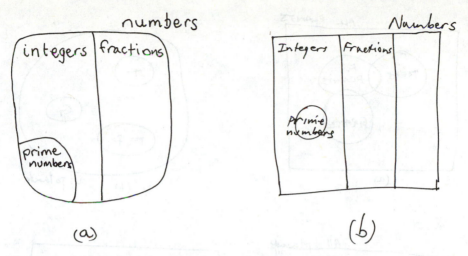

Figure 8.4: Relational diagram for the terms 'integers', 'prime numbers', 'fractions', 'numbers' drawn by (a) a 12-year-old and (b) a university mathematics graduate

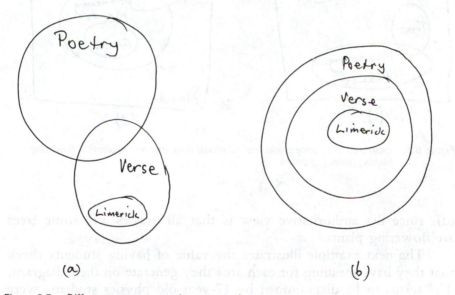

Figure 8.5: Different responses to the same task

exercise in training programs for teachers as well as with secondary school students, so have been able to collect many examples of how relational diagrams reveal understanding about them. The four parts of Figure 8.6 are responses by science graduates. The diagrams demonstrate shortcomings in the understandings of all but person

127

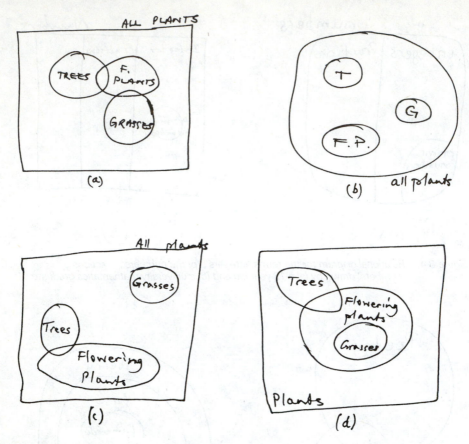

Figure 8.6: *Examples of science graduates' relational diagrams for 'all plants', 'flowering plants', 'trees', 'grasses'*

(d), since the authoritative view is that all grasses and some trees are flowering plants.

The next example illustrates the value of having students check that they have meaning for each area they generate on their diagram. The terms to be diagrammed by 17-year-old physics students were *objects with changing velocity* (given as a starting point, as in step 1 of our suggested instructions), and the two groups *objects with changing acceleration* and *objects with constant (but not zero) acceleration*.

Figure 8.7 shows one student's response. The area marked 'X' on the figure illustrates our point. If this has meaning for the student (that is, it is not just empty space), then the student's understanding of velocity and acceleration is flawed, for it asserts that there can be objects with changing velocity which have neither constant nor

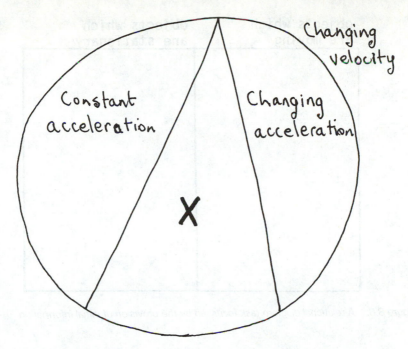

*Figure 8.7: A student's relational diagram with an unlabelled area*

changing acceleration. A subsequent interview established that this was indeed the meaning intended by this student.

Figure 8.8 shows how giving more information at the beginning of the task can focus it on particular relations. The students, 16-year-olds in a physics class, were asked to add to the figure areas for *objects which have a resultant force acting on them* and *objects which have no resultant force acting on them*. The information given in the initial diagram focussed attention on the relations seen between *resultant force* and *motion*. Some of the students' responses are shown in Figure 8.9. Response (a) indicates a belief that moving objects and objects with a resultant force acting are identical groups, as are stationary objects and objects with no resultant force on them. This probably arises from the common erroneous belief that motion implies that a force is acting. Response (b) is a relatively common one from high school students, which omits the recognition present in response (c) that objects can for an instant be stationary while having a resultant force acting (e.g., an object oscillating on a spring when at the extremes of its motion). Response (a) is clearly at odds with physics. Response (b) can also be argued to be incomplete, but might be judged to be quite acceptable for students at many levels of schooling.

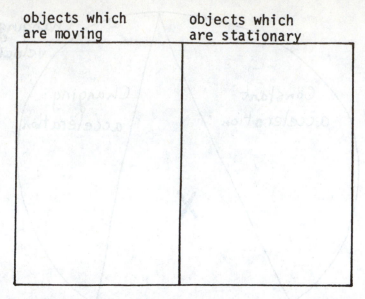

<table>
<tr><td>objects which<br>are moving</td><td>objects which<br>are stationary</td></tr>
</table>

*Figure 8.8: A relational diagram task focussed by the provision of initial information*

Relational diagrams can be used across the whole curriculum, as the following examples show.

Hunters, nomads
Seas, lakes, bodies of fresh water
Sports, games, recreations
Vehicles, cars, ships
Letters, correspondence
Assets, funds
Polygons, quadrilaterals, squares
Fluids, liquids, gases, solids
Sweets, lollies
Maps, plans, scale drawings
Laws, regulations
Criminals, convicts, prisoners
Clothes, shoes
Myths, legends, fables
Plays, farces, tragedies, comedies
Numbers, digits
Facts, opinions, beliefs
Chairs, seats
Punishments, admonishments

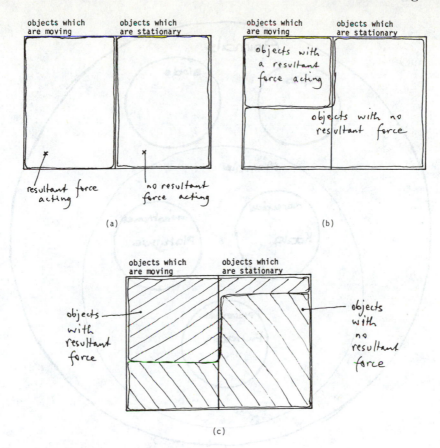

Figure 8.9:   Three student responses

Songs, arias, ballads
Evil people, wicked people, nasty people
Numbers, fractions, surds
Pictures, paintings, photographs
Arguments, disputes, quarrels
Rebellions, revolts, uprisings
Heroic acts, foolish acts
Aims, goals
Students, pupils, scholars
Useful activities, work, teaching
Teaching techniques, testing techniques

It is possible to make a mess of any technique. We include Figure 8.10 to warn against a mistake we made early on, when we were

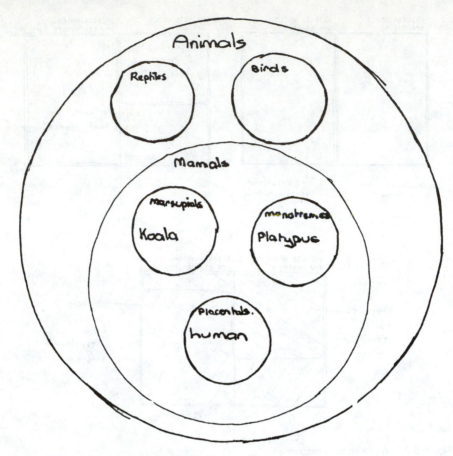

*Figure 8.10:   A relational diagram task with too many terms*

developing the technique. One of us was teaching a grade 7 science class, and asked the students to draw a relational diagram for the terms *animals, mammals, reptiles, birds, marsupials, monotremes, placentals, koala, platypus,* and *human.* The error is that there are too many terms. The example in Figure 8.10 is one of the few that was intelligible. What was worse was that this was the first relational diagram that these 12-year-old students had been asked to do. Even students experienced in relational diagrams would find challenging such a large number of terms, so it is not surprising that the task was difficult for the young, inexperienced students and, probably, put them off relational diagrams for life. The example points to the care needed in determining both the number and nature of terms given for a relational diagram.

### Introducing Relational Diagrams to Students

Begin with a simple diagram that involves concepts that are familiar to the students so they can concentrate on the procedure. That recommendation may appear obvious, but we arrived at it by making the mistake of confronting new students with a difficult example. Suitable terms could be *people*, *males*, and *females*, followed by *adults* and *children*; or *animals*, *meat eaters*, and *vegetable eaters*; or *dogs*, *big dogs*, and *scary dogs*. Note that in each example there is an all-embracing term.

Construct an example yourself in front of the class, working aloud, before setting the students to their first attempt.

For the students' first attempt, guide them through a step-by-step construction:

Draw a big circle to stand for all the people.
Label it *people*.
Now draw a line to cut off part of the circle to take in all the males. Label it.
What will we label the rest of the circle?
(Females). Label it.
Now we are to divide the circle again, between adults and children. Draw a line to show that.

and so on.

### Choosing Terms for a Relational Diagram

Experience leads us to make two recommendations about the choice of terms: first keep the number small, from two to five; and second, try drawing the diagram yourself before asking students to do it.

Where the words in concept maps and word associations can be of almost any form, collections of such different natures as emotions, names of individuals, abstractions, specific objects, and groups of things, the terms in relational diagrams must stand for classes of things or ideas of similar nature. It is pointless to ask for a relational diagram for, say, *atoms*, *universities*, and *war*, though it would be possible for those terms to be linked in a concept map or through word association.

Each term in a relational diagram will be plural, since it stands for a set of instances. A singular term appears only as a specific case, representing a region of the diagram but not as a rule constituting an

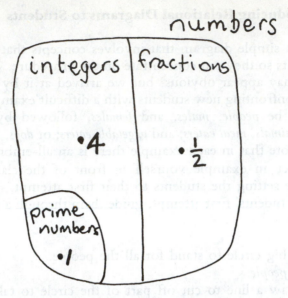

*Figure 8.11: Specific instances added to a relational diagram*

area by itself. There can be exceptions to this rule, for instance the Governor-General could have been given a separate area all to himself in Figure 8.1, since he can be regarded as a third part of the Australian parliament along with the two houses; or the number 1 could be given a spot in Figure 8.4 since it is an integer that is neither prime nor factorisable.

## Variations and Extensions

### 1. Placing Specific Cases

After the diagram is completed, ask the students to mark on it where one or more specific instances would fit. For the numbers diagram of Figure 8.4, they were asked to place *1, 4,* and *1/2*; the 12-year-old's response shown in Figure 8.11 shows that he regards *1* as a prime, contrary to mathematicians' definition.

We confessed earlier to giving too many terms to a year 7 class (Figure 8.10). It would have been better to have given at first only the terms *animals, birds, reptiles, mammals, marsupials, monotremes,* and *placentals* (though this would still have been too many), and then asked the students to mark in *koala, platypus,* and *human* as specific cases.

Further examples of terms for which relational diagrams can be drawn, with specific cases, are:

| General terms | Specific cases |
| --- | --- |
| books, novels, biographies | *Ivanhoe; Hitler: A Study in Tyranny; The Bible* |
| sports, games, recreations | table tennis; walking; chess, Monopoly; reading |
| machines, tools | spanner; needle; scissors; electric saw; crane |
| legal actions, just actions, wise actions | Ford's pardoning of Nixon; Kerr's dismissal of Whitlam; Baldwin's requirement that Edward VIII renounce either Mrs Simpson or the throne |
| myths, legends, fables | Robin Hood; The Golden Fleece; Uncle Remus |

### 2  *Providing Specific Cases*

In this extension, students are required to name a specific case for designated areas of their diagram. A teacher might normally require one example for each area, so that for Figure 8.6(d) five examples would be needed. If the students write the examples on the appropriate space in the diagram, it is obvious when some areas are left unexemplified, which can spur the student to revise the diagram.

The examples the students put forward provide a further probe of their understanding. It is not uncommon to find that a student who has drawn a correct diagram will suggest examples that demonstrate lack of understanding.

### 3  *Provoked Revision*

Some misunderstandings, or mis-drawings, are so common that one can foresee them occurring with a class and so can devise specific cases that will force students to reconsider their relational diagrams. This extension is more directed at teaching better understanding than at probing.

The drawings in Figure 8.12 are an example. The students are given the two rectangles side-by-side, marked high and low resistance. Their task is:

135

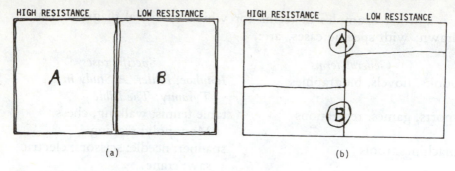

Figure 8.12: *Responses revealing different levels of understanding*

Consider situations where we connect wires, or objects containing wires (e.g. light globes) to a 1.5 joule/coulomb cell. The wires can be divided into high resistance and low resistance

On the diagram you have been given, show:

A — situations where *a lot* of electric potential energy is converted to heat and/or light
B — situations where only *a little* electric potential energy is converted to heat and/or light

We find that high school students and even science graduates often produce drawings like that of Figure 8.12(a), when 8.12(b) would be better. When that happens, challenge them to think further about the relation between resistance and energy conversion by asking them to complete the six tasks of Figure 8.13.

The first three tasks of Figure 8.13 are relatively straightforward, and students whose diagrams are like that of Figure 8.12(a) have little trouble with them. But the second three were chosen to challenge 8.12(a) diagrams and so to provoke revision by the students.

The respondents' ability to make appropriate changes to their initial diagrams is a further indication of understanding, so an explicit instruction is given to them to reconsider the first drawing. A further extension is to ask them to write the reasons for changing or not changing their diagrams.

Even if the examples you gave were not intended to provoke revision, they may have that effect on some students. Therefore we

Now mark points on the diagram to represent each of the following six

particular cases:

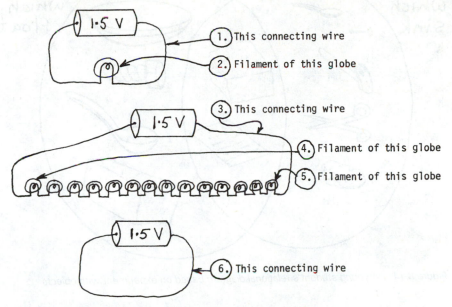

1. This connecting wire
2. Filament of this globe
3. This connecting wire
4. Filament of this globe
5. Filament of this globe
6. This connecting wire

*Figure 8.13:    Specific instances to be placed on a relational diagram in order to provoke
student reflection*

advise always encouraging students to check whether they need to
revise their diagrams in the light of the example-locating tasks.

### 4    Contrasting

Figure 8.1 showed a student's representation of relations among members of the Australian parliament. Similarities and differences that the
student perceives between the Australian and United States legislative
systems are shown clearly if in addition you ask them to draw a
relational diagram for members of the US *Congress, House of Representatives, Senate,* and *Cabinet.* That may be seen as more of a teaching
application than a probe of understanding. It does show the efficiency
of relational diagrams, when one considers that an alternative
approach would be to ask students to write about the similarities and
differences of the two systems. Although there is more opportunity in
an essay to bring out fine points, the pair of relational diagrams makes
the students' understanding of the fundamental features of the two
systems immediately apparent.

137

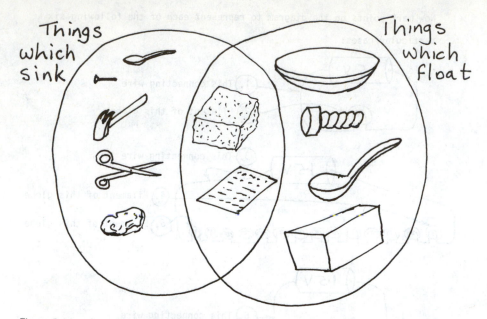

Figure 8.14: *A young student's relational diagram based on experiment with objects*

### 5  Summarising Activities

Sometimes it is useful to check on the understanding students have of a sorting activity. Some 7-year-olds, for instance, had a lesson in which they placed objects in water to see which floated and which sank. Afterwards they were asked to group cut-out drawings of the objects to show what happened. Figure 8.14 shows one student's response.

The student's classification included two objects which floated for a while, but then sank. Hence she had the two groups overlapping. She placed the bowl in the floating group, even though she had turned it on its side so it then sank, because she had had to make it sink. The sponge and newspaper, shown in the intersection of the two groups, had eventually sunk without interference.

### What the Procedure Reveals

Relational diagrams show the meanings that people give to terms that stand for classes of objects. The principal target is understanding of

138

concepts. However, the diagrams are also probes of understanding of single elements of knowledge. The diagram of Figure 8.8 and the responses shown in Figure 8.9 amount to a probe of understanding of a proposition, Newton's second law of motion. Also the extension to requiring placement of specific cases is a test of understanding of a single element: placing Mussolini on a diagram for *demagogues*, *dictators*, and *tyrants* requires knowledge of specific facts about Mussolini.

## Scoring of Relational Diagrams

Although for some terms (e.g., *honest people*, *politicians*) the best form of relational diagram is a matter of opinion, in most cases where they are used there will be an authoritatively correct form. The latter type, if it suits the teacher's purpose, can be marked right or wrong, and a score given that corresponds to the degree of similarity with the correct version. Even the former can be given a subjective rating. Most often, though, we believe that teachers will use relational diagrams for diagnosis rather than summative assessment, and there will be no need to assign a score.

## Using Relational Diagrams in Teaching

The conciseness and precision of relational diagrams make them useful in explaining, and their simple visual structure makes it easier for students to comprehend the explanation and to remember the result. Imagine, for instance, a teacher trying to explain the relation between odes and sonnets, or surds and irrational numbers. This can be done with words, but the processing of those words by the students is not simple. Probably more will fail to grasp the distinction than would if the teacher drew a relational diagram.

Relational diagrams are useful in instigating and focussing discussion, with a class or an individual student, in order to get students to clarify their meanings for terms or even to alter their beliefs about issues that are important to them.

A teacher to whom we had shown relational diagrams had a student with muscular dystrophy, a serious and progressive disease that had left the student with limited motor skills. The student had been shifted from a school for the disabled to a mainstream secondary school, and was finding it difficult to adjust to his new circumstances. The teacher asked him to draw a relational diagram for the terms *people*, *disabled people*, and *disabled children*. The diagram promoted discussion between them, in which the teacher's initial purpose was to encourage the student to understand that he was thinking of disabled in a narrow way limiting it to extreme physical or intellectual disability. The teacher used the diagram to show him that her notion of disability was broad, that most people have some form of disability. The student then asked what her main disability was (poor eyesight), and then talked with her about the degree of handicap that led people to be classed as disabled. This single episode did not result in a dramatic reappraisal by the student of his circumstances, but it did trigger a willingness to think and talk about them which he had resisted previously.

With class teaching, the rapid assessment that a diagram allows facilitates discussion between teacher and student. Essays inhibit discussion because they take too long for the teacher to read, but the teacher can respond quickly to a diagram. Moving around the class, the teacher can inspect a diagram in a second, ask a question to probe more deeply or to get the student to think further, and move on to the next student in far less time than it would take with a written answer.

Discussion between students can be fostered by having them work in groups to produce relational diagrams. Arguments about how to represent the classes of terms will bring out different views and will train students to defend their ideas and to evaluate those of other people.

## Nomenclature

The usual name for relational diagrams is Venn diagrams. We avoid that term because many students, and, probably, teachers too, who have experienced Venn diagrams in mathematics classes have developed an antipathy to them. We feel it would be a pity if so useful and enjoyable a technique were resisted because of negative associations with its name.

## Further Reading

Some of the ideas presented in this chapter appeared in two journal articles:

GUNSTONE, R.F. and WHITE, R.T. (1983) 'Testing and teaching with Venn diagrams', *Australian Science Teachers Journal*, **29**, 3, pp. 63–4.

GUNSTONE, R.F. and WHITE, R.T. (1986) 'Assessing understanding by means of Venn diagrams', *Science Education*, **70**, pp. 151–58.

The latter paper mentions non-mathematical uses of Venn diagrams such as clarifying the descriptors used in computer searches of library holdings, clarifying the meaning of terms in a doctoral thesis, and in the teaching of chemistry.

## Chapter 9

# Word Association

Word association is a direct probe of the associations that a person perceives for a set of concepts. Normally the concepts will be key terms in a topic or discipline. People are asked to give series of one-word responses to the terms. Figure 9.1 shows the responses that a 19-year-old fine arts student gave to key words from the topic of ceramics.

### Purposes of Word Association

In Chapter 1 understanding was identified with the number and nature of the relations that a person perceives between elements of knowledge. If we could find out those relations, we would have insight into the quality of the person's understanding of the elements. Word association is a procedure designed to elicit the relations people have formed between concepts. As concepts can be units within topics, word association can be used to measure understanding not only of concepts themselves but also of whole disciplines, of situations, and even of people.

The numbers and types of responses that people give to key terms are interpreted to assess their understanding of a topic. The interpretation is subjective, even when you assign numerical values. One might judge the responses in Figure 9.1, for example, as revealing a moderate extent of knowledge. However, there is no evidence of understanding of the scientific basis of ceramics, which together with the absence of responses from other arts or from history or from applications of ceramics suggests that the topic is understood as isolated and largely experiential knowledge. For instance, responses such as T'ang dynasty, celadon, particle size, sintering, superconductors,

**CERAMICS**

| *kiln* | *wheel* | *clay* | *glaze* | *coils* | *pottery* |
|---|---|---|---|---|---|
| heat | circle | mud | glass | snakes | clay |
| element | spinning | shape | colour | clay | selling |
| firing | | pots | firing | building | |
| electricity | | | waterproofing | | |
| gas | | | chemicals | | |
| glazes | | | | | |
| bricks | | | | | |

| *porcelain* | *oxide* | *kaolin* |
|---|---|---|
| fine | colour | chemical |
| light | pencil | glazes |
| translucent | red | flux |
| white | | |
| smooth | | |

Figure 9.1:    Associations given by fine arts student to stimulus words (shown here in italics) after being told that the topic is ceramics

insulators, elegance and form would give a different impression of quality of understanding. There is also little overlap between responses to words, suggesting that the student has yet to integrate the topic.

As well as subjective judgements about a single set of responses, word association can be used to chart changes in an individual's understanding, to compare the understandings of people or groups, or to compare a person's understanding with a standard such as the connections that a textbook specifies between concepts.

## Procedure

A major advantage of word association tests is that they are simple to prepare and to give. They are almost as easy to give to large numbers of students as to an individual. The central part of the procedure is to present the stimulus words one at a time to the students, who write a series of single word responses to each stimulus, continuing each series until they run dry of responses or until the teacher directs them to move on to the next stimulus.

### Materials

Although many variations of materials are possible, a practical form is a pad of sheets for each student, each sheet bearing 10 to 15 repetitions

IMPRESSIONISM

Impressionism _____

Impressionism _____

Impressionism _____

Impressionism _____

Impressionism _____

Impressionism _____

Impressionism _____

Impressionism _____

Impressionism _____

Impressionism _____

*Figure 9.2: Example of word association sheet*

of one stimulus word with spaces for the student to write responses (see Figure 9.2).

### Steps

1   The teacher begins with a preamble. A possible form is: 'This is a test to see how many words you can think of in a short time. You will be given some key words. For each key word write all the words it makes you think of. If you do not fill all the spaces provided, do not worry; just put in as many words as you can. Put only one word on each line.'
2   'Turn to the first sheet on the pad. The key word is [    ].'
3   The teacher judges when to move the students on to the next word, either by passage of a pre-determined interval or, more likely, by seeing that most students have stopped writing. In our experience, one minute is a practical interval for secondary and tertiary students. 'Turn to the next sheet. The key word is [    ].'
4   When all the key words have been responded to, the teacher collects the pads for later analysis of the responses.

### Introducing Word Association to Students

Because the procedure is straightforward and the task for the students is simple, we have experienced no problems, nor have had any reported to us, in the introduction of word association to students. One can almost leap in with a minimum of explanation. However, explanation, practice, and feedback will make the early experiences more effective.

*1 Explanation* You might tell the students that the purpose of word association is to see what ideas they link together in their minds. Say 'I am going to say a word, and I want you to write down the first word that comes into your head. Ready? *Snake.*' Check that all have written a word, read out some examples, and make it clear that all responses are satisfactory. Then, 'Now write another word when I say *snake*'. 'And now another, *snake.*'

Next show the students a completed response list, such as Figure 9.1, pointing out its features.

*2 Practice* Give the students a simple exercise, with about three or four stimulus words for common objects, e.g., *cow, horse, sheep.* Discuss their efforts.

*3 Feedback* Follow the first few uses of the technique with a report on performance.

## Variations and Extensions

A disadvantage of word association is that the responses are sensitive to variations in procedure. A different preamble, a different mode of presentation of the stimulus words, or a different layout of the response sheets can change what the students record. In determining the details of procedure, the teacher will consider the purpose of the test and the familiarity of the students with word association.

In our experience, the more familiar the students are with word association, the less the details of the preamble or layout matter. The students develop a standard procedure of their own for responding to the test. However, it is possible to influence their responses by emphasising certain points in the preamble. Compare, for instance, the following extracts from preambles:

A 'For example, suppose I asked an electrician to write down as many words relating to electricity (his specialty) as he could think of when given the word *Conductor*. He might put down the following:

*Conductor*

| | | | |
|---|---|---|---|
| Conductor | metal | Conductor | resistor |
| Conductor | charge | Conductor | |
| Conductor | transmit | Conductor | |

You will notice that as an electrician, he did not put *train* or *cable car* or *guide*, since they do not relate to the electrical concept of *conductor*. In this same way, you should think like a physicist when you response to the concepts.'

B  'You should try to think of as many different sorts of things as you can. Do not just stick to the same topic. For example, for the word *Napoleon* think not only of his battles but also you could respond *brandy* or *cakes* or *laws*.'

Extract A directs the students to keep within the bounds of a limited topic, while B tries to see whether they have formed links with widely diverse topics. The notion of understanding explored in A is of completeness of knowledge within the topic, and in B of integration of the topic with a broader sweep of knowledge.

Variations in layout of response sheets can influence the responses. In Figure 9.2 the stimulus word was repeated, when it might seem simpler to use it once only, at the head of the page. The reason for repeating it is to minimise the effect of chaining, in which the previous response rather than the key word becomes the stimulus for the next response. Thus if the key word is *golf*, a response *club* could lead to the next responses being *spade* then *garden*, a chain that is leading away to more distant knowledge. By repeating *golf* on each line the responses should be kept close to the stimulus of interest.

Another variation is whether the key words are presented one at a time or all together on a single large sheet. We prefer the former, since presenting all the words at once means that the responses are really an amalgam of the influences of the whole set of stimuli not just to the key word under which the person places them. However, the responses to one-stimulus-at-a-time are not absolutely independent either, after the first stimulus. Responses to *club* may well be different if the previous stimulus was *golf* than if it was *heart* or *league*. This means that the sequence of presentation of the stimulus words affects responses. There are no rules for determining sequence, but it should be appreciated that when the more specific and less ambiguous words come first there will be greater coherence in the responses than when they come last. 'Struggle — battle — Alamein — Montgomery' is likely to see less overlap between struggle and Montgomery than if the order were reversed.

The number of spaces on the response sheet will also have an effect, since students will infer that that is the number of responses they should make. With a large number of spaces the later responses for each word may be more random than real associations. It is hard to say how many spaces should be given. We have found that ten is satisfactory with junior secondary school students.

Although variations in preamble and layout can affect responses, they do not constitute an extension or significant improvement of the word association technique. The only substantial improvement of which we are aware is Gunstone's (1980) requirement that, after making the last response, for each response the person writes a sentence that shows a relation between it and the stimulus word. Thus after responding to *channel* with *safety* a person wrote, 'The English Channel provided Britain with a margin of safety in wartime.' This requirement goes some way towards overcoming a weakness of word association that Stewart (1979) pointed out, that the basic method tells you only that the person associates two concepts and leaves you in the dark about the nature of the association. Imagine that three people respond to the stimulus *sultana* with *Turkey*; their understandings are not the same if their sentences are 'Sultana was the title for the queen of Turkey', 'Sultanas come from grapes that are grown in Turkey', and 'My favourite food is turkey with sultana stuffing'.

Gunstone's improvement has the disadvantage of requiring more time, and tends to inhibit the readiness of students to respond. It is less convenient to use with young children, who may have trouble in constructing sentences. Its use in preference to the basic procedure will depend on whether the teacher wants a quick survey of responses to a substantial number of terms, say eight or more, or a deeper look at the relations students see among a few specially important ones.

Word association as we have described it permits free response. A related but circumscribed procedure would be to give students lists of words and ask them to cluster them into groups. The number of groups can be specified or left open. Imagine you were asked to place the following composers in, say, five groups: Beethoven Brahms Bruckner Grieg Handel Haydn Mahler Mozart Nielsen Purcell Schubert Schumann Wagner. Your response should reveal something of your understanding of music. It would be even more revealing if you had to describe the principles behind your groupings.

A further variation of this clustering procedure would be to mix terms from three or four topics, have students read them, then after a brief interval ask them to write as many of the terms as they can recall. Many researchers have used this procedure to measure the degree of organization the individual has applied to the list, which they measure by seeing how often words from the same topic appear together. A respondent who as often puts in sequence words from unconnected as connected topics is not organizing the list at all. Another interpretation is that that person has little understanding of the topics. As far as we know, teachers have not used this procedure, though for a period it was popular among researchers. It could be useful from time to time.

### What the Procedure Reveals

To some extent word association does the same job as concept mapping (Chapter 2), in that both provide patterns of links between concepts. There are, however, important differences.

Word association is much more managed than concept mapping, and consequently is less fun for students. It lacks the physical and social activity of mapping. In a concept map the student constructs directly the pattern of relations, but in word association the teacher deduces it from complex analysis of the word lists. The teacher does most of the construction, and the student may never see the derived pattern of associations. Consequently there is much less opportunity for the student to learn from taking part in a word association test than there is in doing a concept map. Further, because word association is an individual response while concept maps can be done by groups, word association provokes less discussion and so is a less powerful teaching technique. Perhaps these reasons explain why word association is less popular, in our experience, with teachers and students.

If word association had only disadvantages when compared with concept mapping, there would be no reason to use it at all. However, it does have positive features, of which the chief is the ease with which the lists of responses can be turned into quantitative values that provide summary measures of understanding.

In the section below on scoring we describe how three features of response lists can be given scores: the number and type of responses and the overlap between pairs of lists. The number of responses that a word receives is an important and direct indication of the person's understanding of it, since meaning can be defined as being proportional to the number of links the person can make to the word. A word for which the person can make no links must be meaningless to that person. Of course, in interpreting the number of responses a student makes to a stimulus word, the teacher must be sensitive to differences between students in their fluency or readiness to state associations. While some are quick to blurt forth response after response with little thought, more hesitant or reflective students will pause and filter what they say. Therefore caution is needed in making comparisons between people.

Less caution is required in inferring differences in understanding between terms, either within one person's set of responses or across those of a whole group of students. Thus if Joan gives eight responses to the cue *sonata* while Ian gives four, it is not immediately certain that Joan knows more about, and understands better, *sonata* than Ian does. You would have to know more about the general levels of response that Joan and Ian make before you could infer anything from the eight and four. However, if Joan made only two responses to *arpeggio* it is reasonable to judge that she has a more extensive understanding of *sonata* than of *arpeggio*. Further, if the class averages several times as many responses to *sonata* than to *arpeggio*, the teacher might well infer that they understand *sonata* better. Even in making cross-term comparisons, however, caution is necessary because some terms may be intrinsically more linkable than others. A large number of links may indicate that understanding of the term is extensive but diffuse, while a small number might show that it is limited but precise. To be sure of whether that is the case or whether large means extensive, specific and rich while small means poor and vague, further probing by interview would be necessary.

Types of responses and overlap between lists may be more interesting than simple total numbers of responses, since they can tell about the nature of the person's understanding. When similar responses are made to all the stimulus words, a possible interpretation is that the person has integrated the topic well. However, lack of responses from other fields may show a narrow understanding, a failure to relate the topic to wider knowledge. Close similarities of responses to subsets of the stimulus words may indicate that the person understands the topic as a collection of poorly integrated sub-topics. We would not want to push that inference too far, since in our experience people do not tend to give strongly overlapping responses even when other probes indicate that their understanding is good. Figure 9.3 shows associations that an adult made to names of four important

| William Bligh | Arthur Phillip | Matthew Flinders | James Cook |
|---|---|---|---|
| rum | governor | Donington | captain |
| mutiny | Australia | Anne | Australia |
| Fletcher Christian | Bath | navigator | Hawaii |
| Charles Laughton | portrait | Australia | Endeavour |
| Timor Sea | | Mauritius | Banks |
| bed | | boats | Straights |
| | | Bass | shipwreck |
| | | street | islands |
| | | Partney | university |
| | | Lincolnshire | Cooktown |

*Figure 9.3:   Associations to four figures in Australian history, given by an adult*

figures in Australian history. There is hardly any overlap, though we know from long discussions with the respondent that she has considerable knowledge of the period and, we judge, a fine understanding.

One might expect greater overlap if the test were given immediately following a course of instruction, but even then it could be slight. Shavelson (1972) reports relatedness coefficients (see section on scoring) that rose during six days of instruction from a mean of zero to 0.32.

The sequence of responses also tells something about understanding, if one presumes that the first words that come to mind are more closely associated than later ones with the stimulus word. In Figure 9.3 one would then infer that the respondent sees Bligh and rum as more closely associated than Bligh and the Timor Sea.

Inferences about understanding that are made from the response lists are subjective, and remain so even when scores are given to features such as number of responses per stimulus and overlap between pairs of lists. A simple test of knowledge that took about as much time as the word association test could check more directly whether knowledge had been gained, and because it might be seen as less subjective might seem to remove the need to ever use word association. Such a test would not, however, yield the same information nor have the same effect on learning. The key difference is that the word association test is open, allowing students to reveal links that they have made between the topic being assessed and other knowledge, while the knowledge test is closed, requiring specific responses. Word association emphasises links between concepts, while the knowledge test treats all items as separate. Occasional exposure to word association might bring students to appreciate the need to reflect on the interlinking of topics, and so can promote superior habits of learning.

### Scoring of Word Association

Shavelson (1974) asserts that although there are diverse ways of scoring word association tests, all reduce the richness of the response lists — an observation that is pertinent to all probes of understanding and indeed to tests generally. However, the prevailing expectation in education is that tests will yield scores, so we must consider how the response lists can be converted to numbers.

Shavelson notes that word association sets have three properties: the number of responses to each stimulus word, the nature of these responses, and the overlap between responses to pairs of words. All three properties can be converted to scores.

#### Number of Words

An obvious property of a person's responses is the total number of associations listed. It is reasonable to assume that the greater the number the better the understanding, though it should be recognised that the layout of the response sheet may constrain the number, and that the number is also a function of the person's fluency. A cautious, reticent person may write fewer responses than a careless, glib one, despite having a better understanding. Research results are consistent with the equivocal character of number of responses as a measure of understanding, with some (e.g., Johnson, 1967, 1969) finding a positive correlation with achievement and others (e.g., Shavelson, 1973) finding no connection.

If, despite these cautions, you want to use number of responses as a measure of understanding, the scoring is simple: just count how many the person made.

Another property of number of responses is their distribution across the stimulus words. The two sets of responses in Figure 9.4 have the same total of responses, 30, but the distributions are markedly different, reflecting differences in quality of understanding.

How one interprets differences such as those apparent in Figure 9.4 is debatable. Is it better if the pattern is uneven, or worse? For practical purposes of class teaching, it may be sufficient to note the pattern, and decide whether the student needs to learn more about specific concepts in the topic or to learn more about all of them.

If you want to sum the pattern of distribution by a single score, any of the common statistical measures of dispersion such as standard deviation, range, or inter-quartile range would do. Our own view is

| Merchant of Venice | Othello | King Lear | Macbeth | Midsummer Night's Dream |
|---|---|---|---|---|
| injustice | Iago | daughters | murder | Bottom |
| Shylock | smothering | blinding | Duncan | Regent's Park |
| Portia | | | witches | love |
| caskets | | | spot | play-in-play |
| suitors | | | Lady Macbeth | |
| pound of flesh | | | ghost | |
| Daniel | | | dinner | |
| arrogance | | | Banquo | |
| usury | | | McDuff | |
| Rialto | | | porter | |
| | | | wood | |
| | | | thane | |

| Merchant of Venice | Othello | King Lear | Macbeth | Midsummer Night's Dream |
|---|---|---|---|---|
| Shylock | moor | ingratitude | witches | ass's head |
| money lending | treachery | Cordelia | blasted heath | Titania |
| Bassanio | jealousy | James Thurber | cauldron | Bottom |
| Portia | tupping | age | murder | wall |
| Jew | prejudice | folly | ambition | lion |
| pound of flesh | death | | hen-pecked | Mendelssohn |
| | | | ghost | |

*Figure 9.4: Two sets of responses to same stimulus words, illustrating unevenness and evenness of spread*

that such statistical precision is unnecessary — inspection of the pattern and subjective evaluation will be more useful to the classroom teacher.

### Type of Response

In scoring a set of responses for type, the teacher will have in mind categories of associations. One type of category that we have been interested in is whether the response is a term that we judge would have been presented in teaching as a concept that is part of the topic, or whether it is one from outside the topic. Because of our acceptance of Arthur Koestler's notion that creative people see links between apparently unrelated topics (Koestler, 1964), we have regarded outside associations as positive. An opposing assessment might be that outside associations reflect disorganised knowledge or random listing, and should be penalised. So it is up to the teacher to decide not only the types of response that are to be looked at but which types indicate good understanding.

To arrive at a score, one simple procedure would be to determine the percentage of responses that are in the categories.

| BASEBALL | 7 | CRICKET | 6 |
|----------|---|---------|---|
| run | 6 | run | 5 |
| bat | 5 | wicket | 4 |
| field | 4 | bowl | 3 |
| throw | 3 | field | 2 |
| base | 2 | baseball | 1 |
| bleachers | 1 | | |

*Figure 9.5:   Ranked responses to two terms that overlap slightly*

## Overlap

Suppose a student gives lots of responses that appear sensible to two stimulus words such as *sonata* and *symphony*, yet none of the responses to *sonata* appears in the *symphony* list. Does this reveal anything about the student's understanding of musical forms? Many people might interpret it as an indication of lack of integration of knowledge, therefore overlap between pairs of responses might need to be scored. There are numerous ways of summing overlap into a number, and as none of them is obviously superior teachers must choose the procedure that suits them best.

Consider the responses to *baseball* and *cricket* listed in Figure 9.5. They differ, but the responses *run* and *field* are common to both and *baseball* appears in the cricket list. One way of summing the association between baseball and cricket is to say that three of the words in the shorter list, to *cricket*, which has six words in it if we count cricket itself, appear in the baseball list, so the association is $3 \div 6 = 0.5$. Or we could say that for the two lists combined there are thirteen words and there are six (three pairs) words common to both so the index is $6 \div 13 = 0.46$.

Shavelson (1972) used a more sophisticated index, the Relatedness Coefficient (RC) developed by Garskoff and Houston (1963). This coefficient takes into account the rank order of responses. The ranks for the words are the numbers beside them in Figure 9.5. The formula for the coefficient is:

$$RC = \frac{\text{Sum of products of ranks of common words}}{\Sigma\, n^2 - 1}$$

where n is the number of words in the longer list.

For the baseball–cricket pair, the common words are *baseball* (ranks 7 and 1), *run* (6 and 5), and *field* (4 and 2), and as there are seven words in the longer list n = 7. Hence

$$RC = \frac{(7 \times 1) + (6 \times 5) + (4 \times 2)}{7^2 + 6^2 + 5^2 + 4^2 + 3^2 + 2^2 + 1^2 - 1} = \frac{45}{139} = 0.32$$

The index is not as satisfactory as its complexity might imply. Its top value of 1.0 is attained when two lists are identical, but this can occur for very short lists as well as for long. People might feel there is stronger association when two long lists of responses are identical than when there is only a word or two in each list. The index is also sensitive to the sequence of the responses, so that if *run* had been placed lower in either or both lists the RC value would have been smaller.

Our final comment on scoring, whether of number or type of responses or of overlap, is that the procedure followed depends on the purpose and preference of the user, and that in any case the numbers have to be interpreted. Subjectivity enters into that interpretation. Our own preference is not to reduce the response lists to numbers, but to inspect them thoroughly and to form a composite judgement about the quality of understanding that each set reveals. Teachers may find our approach as useful as any sophisticated numerical analysis.

## Using Word Association in Teaching

Although word association may appear less applicable as a teaching procedure than other probes that readily provoke discussion, such as concept maps and relational diagrams, some useful extensions are possible. For instance, the teacher may ask all the students in a class to construct a sentence that links a given pair of concepts. The class can then compare and discuss the sentences: Who else in the class would have thought of such a link? Does everyone agree with it? This procedure can be especially useful when one of the concepts is not an obvious part of the topic, or is a general notion, e.g., Napoleon and justice, steam power and slavery, piezoelectricity and music, for then it can train students to search out external links for their knowledge.

Discussion can also be promoted by having students pair off to compare their response lists. They may then learn that there is more than one way to see things, and can come to appreciate that learning is individual and involves personal construction of meaning. The example shown in Figure 9.6 led the two people involved to see that the first one was thinking of the terms in relation to his work in the hotel industry while the second was thinking as a consumer. Their discussion broadened their understanding.

**Respondent A**

| alcohol | spirits | wine | liqueur | beer |
|---------|---------|------|---------|------|
| customers | pourers | corks | brandy balloon | gas |
| bar | ice | labels | | bubbles |
| bottle | cherries | sediment | | temprite |
| money | | vineyards | | gaynew |
| refrigerator | | grapes | | glasses |
| | | | | pots |
| | | | | money |
| | | | | driptrays |

**Respondent B**

| alcohol | spirits | wine | liqueur | beer |
|---------|---------|------|---------|------|
| ethanol | whisky | claret | benedictine | Fosters |
| methanol | gin | moselle | Tia Maria | hops |
| COOH | distillation | riesling | Drambuie | cans |
| drink | brandy | bottling | Linke | drunks |
| intoxication | alcohol | Yarra Glen | ice cream | football |
| excise | rum | drink | cherry brandy | bar |
| | Bundaberg | red | cognac | |
| | ouzo | white | ti toki | |
| | | taste | | |
| | | spritzig | | |

*Figure 9.6:   Contrasting responses that promoted discussion and broadening of both
respondents' understandings*

|  |  |
|---|---|
| Number in class | 28 |

*Exploration of America*

|  |  |
|---|---|
| Columbus | 28 |
| Erickson | 16 |
| Lewis & Clark | 12 |
| Spanish fathers | 4 |
| Ponce de Leon | 3 |
| Henry Hudson | 2 |
| Cabot | 2 |
| Indians | 1 |

*Figure 9.7:   Number of students in class to make specific responses to stimulus 'Exploration
of America' (constructed example)*

A summary of the class responses can be the focus of teaching
and discussion. The teacher can list the numbers of students to make
each link, and can use the results to comment on their understanding.
Suppose the summary for the stimulus *Exploration of America* was as in
Figure 9.7. The teacher could use this to point out the limited nature
of most students' notions of exploration, especially the ethnocentricity
involved in the ignoring of the Indians and the concentration on
Central and North America.

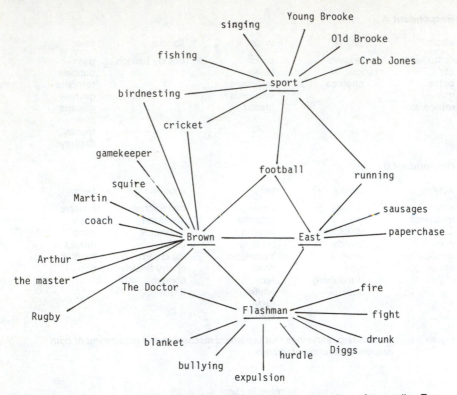

*Figure 9.8:* Summary representation of all associations made by a class after reading Tom Brown's Schooldays

Another form of summary that can be useful as a means of consolidation of knowledge is for the class, or groups within the class, to merge their responses into a chart that depicts all the links that the students made. Figure 9.8 summarises the responses made by a class after reading *Tom Brown's Schooldays*, in response to the four stimulus words *Brown, East, Flashman,* and *sport*. The chart is a permanent reminder to the students of the links that they saw, and also encourages them to search out links in new topics.

## Further Reading

There are hardly any recent accounts of application of word association in education, but up to 1975 it was used frequently by researchers, among whom Richard Shavelson was prominent. His 1974 article, 'Methods for examining representations of a subject-matter structure in a student's memory', which appeared in the *Journal of Research in Science Teaching*, **11**, pp. 231–49, contains a useful discussion of word association and an extensive reference list. Earlier works by Paul Johnson and James Deese are helpful, too:

DEESE, J. (1962) 'On the structure of associative meaning', *Psychological Review*, **69**, pp. 161–75.
JOHNSON, P.E. (1964) 'Associative meaning of concepts in physics', *Journal of Educational Psychology*, **55**, pp. 84–8.

Peter Preece reviewed word association and related methods:

PREECE, P.F.W. (1976) 'Mapping cognitive structure: A comparison of methods', *Journal of Educational Psychology*, **68**, pp. 1–8.

*Chapter 10*

# Question Production

A class of Australian 12-year-olds is learning about the First Fleet and the initial European settlement at Sydney Cove in 1788. In the middle of a discussion of the difficulties facing that settlement, a student asks: 'But why was it the British who settled here?' Questions like this, often unexpected and often insightful, will sometimes occur in any classroom at any level where students feel able to initiate ideas. The questions indicate that the students have been thinking about the ideas being presented in the lesson, and have been trying to extend and link them with other things they know. The questions also reveal much about the students' understanding.

These sorts of questions may occur too rarely. They are also unpredictable. Most teachers would find it much easier to predict which students might ask such questions than to predict when they will ask them. This unpredictability means that students' questions rarely play any planned part in teaching and assessment. This chapter advances ways to rectify this situation by describing strategies which encourage students to ask questions. Once questions become common, teachers can plan to build on them to promote and monitor learning.

The focus of this chapter differs a little from that of the previous ones. Most of the other techniques we have described ask students to respond to a specific task, as they do in conventional tests, but in an unusual form such as concept maps, fortune lines and so on. Students have to be taught how to generate this different product. But with questions the product is anything but unusual. It is hard to imagine students who are unfamiliar with questions, even insightful and probing questions of the form we want to promote. Hence there is less concern here with product and a strong emphasis on process, on strategies for encouraging students to produce questions.

## Purposes of Question Production

Consider your own forming of questions in teaching, both oral ones in class and written ones for tests. Do you find it easier to generate questions when you understand the content well? Which are easier to generate — questions requiring recall of information you have taught, or questions requiring a reframing or application or extension of taught ideas; questions which require students to apply knowledge to explaining or discussing something you see as an example of that knowledge, or questions requiring students to extend knowledge into areas which are new to them?

The point should be clear. By and large, the better your understanding the more readily you will construct questions, and construction of more probing questions (or 'thinking questions' as we prefer to call them in this context) demands more of your understanding. This is because the framing of thinking questions requires you to consider content in different ways. Imagine as an extreme case someone whose knowledge about a topic is only in a linear sequence of ideas in the order they were taught. Such a person could ask recall questions only.

We have phrased the above arguments in the context of teachers asking questions, but they apply equally to students, and illustrate the purposes we see in having students produce questions. We do not want to imply that there are no differences between teachers and students. One difference is that question production, particularly of thinking questions, is not a usual student role, and this has important implications which we discuss in the section below on 'Introducing Question Production to Students'.

## Procedures and Examples

The essence of what is needed for successful promotion of student questions is a way of structuring and focussing the task. Without this, question production will be unpredictable. Here we list five structuring or focussing strategies, and give examples of each.

There are two issues to bear in mind when considering all five strategies. First, the strategy has to be sufficiently open to allow questions that show understanding by extending the ideas that were taught, and not just recall. Second, and closely related to the first, the technique has real value only when students are producing thinking questions rather than questions of less demand. For example, imagine a class studying Australian literature. To have students in that class generate questions of the nature 'Who is the only Australian so far to win the Nobel prize for literature?' will reveal nothing of their understanding of Patrick White as a novelist. However, producing questions such as 'What are the autobiographical emphases in *Voss*?' is a different matter in terms of revealing aspects of understanding of the novelist and his work, assuming of course that the question is not a reproduction of taught material.

### Strategy 1: Ask Students to Begin Questions in a Particular Way

Although questions that demand thought can take almost any form, those that begin with 'What if ...', 'Why does ...', 'Why are ...' or 'How would ...' are more likely to be puzzles than simple recall.

Our first examples are questions asked by 15-year-olds in a commerce subject who had been studying elementary legal issues. This was the first occasion on which they had been asked to generate questions. The instructions given by the teacher began with a task involving review of material covered in class ('Explain what it is we have been studying for the last two weeks and list as much information as you can about the topics covered'.). Then students had to prepare two questions about the work which they would like clarified. The questions were to begin with any of 'What if ...?', 'Why are ...?', 'How would ...?'. Figure 10.1 contains a selection of what they wrote.

The questions in Figure 10.1 cover a wide range, from essentially factual to quite complex and difficult questions. Some questions refer to a sheet of information and issues about the law and one's neighbours which the teacher had used in a previous class. Others relate to personal interests, for example the question about lower driving ages in another Australian state. It is notable, and common in use of this strategy, that not all of the questions begin with one of the four given structures. Of course this does not matter, since other structures which have been used by students, such as 'If ... then what ...?' and 'How come ...?', also result in questions calling for thought.

The questions in Figure 10.2 are from 12-year-olds who had been studying the history of Melbourne. They were asked to 'Make up two questions of your own about the things you've read in the booklet. One should begin with "why" and one with "what if?"'. The proportion of factual questions, opposed to thinking questions, was somewhat greater than the examples in Figure 10.2 suggest.

- Why are the elderly people's pensions stopped if they have over $140,000 even if the assets are just laying there and not earning them an income, e.g., large house?
- Where can you go to find out about all of the laws that are not covered at school?
- How would a person go about learning of the laws and their rights if not at school? Is there a place which records these matters and puts them on display for the public?
- Why are people brought up on many different charges at the same time (e.g., murder, assault, rape, etc.) when they could simply be tried for the most serious one?
- If you can't be committed of a crime between the ages of 8–14, then what is there to stop this age group going on a crime rampage? If a group of 12 year olds smashed the windows of every house and shop in Laverton, would it be assumed that they are under the influence of an adult, or would they simply be given a warning, or would they be put in a detention centre?
  N.B. The crime is an exaggeration.
- On the sheet with the bad neighbourhood how could any one person take another to court or complain about the other persons infringement?
- With reference to the sheet on the neighbours, who is in the right and who is in the wrong, for they have all broken the others rights?
- What if a person wants to find out about the law — where would we go?
- How come, if the federal government makes most of the laws, then why can you drive a car when you are 17 when you live in Queensland?
- What if you were climbing across your fence and your neighbour hit you with the broom. You fell on him and he broke his neck. What would happen?
- How would you convince the law that someone has infringed your rights if there was no witnesses?

*Figure 10.1: Questions generated in response to a given structure — a selection from 15-year-olds (from Baird and Mitchell, 1986, p. 215)*

- Why did Batman come to Australia?
- What if we didn't have a government then what would happen?
- What if the aborigines started to fight back and they won? What would our land be like now?
- What if the Gold Rush didn't happen?
- Why did the settlers kill the aborigines when the aborigines were the first ones here?
- Why do people say that some people drowned in Elizabeth Street?
- Why did the Federal Parliament move to Canberra?

*Figure 10.2: Questions generated in response to a given structure — a selection from 12-year-olds (from Baird and Mitchell, 1986, pp. 112–13)*

## Strategy 2: Provide a Stimulus on Which Questions Are to Be Based

Standard forms of questions used in assessment of learning often centre on a given piece of information or set of ideas. This can be a quotation, a table of data, a map, a diagram and so on. In this widely used form of assessment, the questions to which students are to respond are then based in some way on the given information or ideas. This approach can be adapted to student–generated questions: the students have to write questions based on the stimulus instead of answering them.

'Mary and John walked to the shops. Each of them had $10 to spend. First they went to a sweets shop. Mary bought 2 chocolate bars which cost 75 cents each. John bought a bag of jelly beans for 60 cents. Later, Mary bought a toy car which cost $4.50 and John bought a book for $5.99. John was playing with his money and dropped 20 cents. They could not find the 20 cents, so they stopped shopping and walked home.'

This story is going to be used to test how well students can add and subtract money. Write 2 questions about the story which would test this.

*Figure 10.3:   Question-generating task for primary school mathematics*

'Australia began a large-scale immigration program after World War II. In 1947 the population of the country was under 7 million. In 1990 it is over 16 million. Of these 16 million nearly 90% live in cities and towns and about two-thirds live in cities of more than 100,000 people. This means Australia is one of the most urban countries in the world.'

Use this brief demographic description as the basis for a question which would assess understanding of aspects of recent Australian economic history. Explain why your question would assess understanding.

*Figure 10.4:   Question-generating task for senior high school economics*

Figure 10.3 contains our first example of this approach. This task was used with older primary school children. It assumes that students understand that the more demanding the question they produce, the more their teacher values it. Questions of the form 'How much money did John take shopping?' are much less useful than 'How much money did John take home after shopping?' in providing insight into understanding.

The task shown in Figure 10.4 is for senior secondary students of economics. Here a wider set of questions is possible, and also the students are relatively mature, so they have been asked to justify their questions.

The stimulus can be a map, diagram, or chart. Figure 10.5 shows a diagram stimulus. In this case students must also consider, and invent, the data that would be necessary for their question.

The teachers followed a simple procedure to construct the three foregoing examples: they removed the questions from a conventional test item that was based on a diagram or extended text. Figure 10.6 shows the original form from which the task in Figure 10.3 was derived. For the diagram stimulus (Figure 10.5) the teacher removed both the original question and all the information relevant to it in the diagram.

The origin of these three examples illustrates one considerable

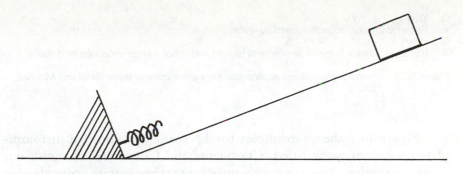

The diagram shows a block on an inclined plane, with a spring at the bottom of the plane. Write a question which is based on the situation in the diagram. If your question requires the values of any relevant quantities, then invent a value for each quantity needed.

*Figure 10.5:   Question-generating task, based on a diagram, for senior high school physics*

'Mary and John walked to the shops. Each of them had $10 to spend. First they went to a sweets shop. Mary bought 2 chocolate bars which cost 75 cents each. John bought a bag of jelly beans for 60 cents. Later, Mary bought a toy car which cost $4.50 and John bought a book for $5.99. John was playing with his money and dropped 20 cents. They could not find the 20 cents, so they stopped shopping and walked home.'

1   How much money did Mary spend?
2   How much money did John take home?

*Figure 10.6:   The original questions used to produce the task shown in Figure 10.3*

advantage of this approach: conventional items provide a ready source of useful stimuli. All you have to do is remove the questions.

*Strategy 3: Provide an Answer and Ask for Questions*

Here we suggest totally reversing the usual process of questioning in order to give another way of focussing student generation of questions. The structure is simple: what question(s) could have the answer ...?

Q.   Why . . . . . . . . . ?
A.   Because Brazil is not surrounded by water.
Q.   Why . . . . . . . . . ?
A.   Because Oceania is made up of lots of islands and is not a large unbroken land mass.

*Figure 10.7:   Generating questions appropriate for a given answer (from Baird and Mitchell, 1986, p. 113)*

Figure 10.7 shows examples for 12-year-olds who had just completed a unit of work titled 'Continents and Countries'. As with our other examples, the students' questions demonstrate considerable variation in the degree of insight into the material just studied. Responses range from factual to complex. The teacher provided the starting word 'Why' for the tasks in Figure 10.7 because this was the first occasion on which these students had been confronted with a question-asking task. For students with a reasonable sense of the purpose of the task such prompts are not necessary. This may result from students having undertaken the task before or, as in our next example, the students being able to grasp the purpose quickly.

Towards the end of in-service sessions with teachers whom we have been teaching concept maps, relational diagrams and so on, we have often asked: What question(s) could have the answer 'Because concept maps show something of the structure an individual places on a set of ideas, and the links the individual sees between some of those ideas'? The responses often reveal the teachers' levels of understanding of concept maps and their uses, and hence give an immediate evaluation of our own teaching.

In this section we have twice written 'question(s)' rather than 'question'. We did that to make the point that the task can easily be extended to require two or more different questions, each of which could have the given answer as an appropriate response. This is more demanding and more revealing than single-question responses.

As with Strategy 2, popular forms of assessment are a source for large numbers of tasks of this form. Take any demanding question from a more traditional context and use an appropriate answer as the beginning point for this task.

We have less experience with applying this strategy to numerical answers, although one of us has been suggesting for many years that Algebra students, used to tasks requiring that they simplify an algebraic expression, would find it more demanding to be asked to 'Complicate $x$'.

It is probably too open-ended to ask students to write questions for which the answer is, say, 42. The technique can work with numerical answers only if you proscribe clearly the content, or the form of the question. For instance, at the end of a series of lessons on decimals, you could ask students to write a question involving the multiplication of two decimal fractions for which the answer is .021, with some hope that the responses would reveal something of the level of the students' understanding.

A procedure we found successful in physics classes is to describe for students the sort of situation that is commonly the preamble in conventional problems: e.g., A 5000 kg truck is travelling at 72 km/hour. The students' task is to write a number of relevant questions, as different as possible, for which the answer is always the same (e.g., 10 seconds). This will involve students in deciding what other concepts, and what values for these concepts, should be introduced.

We think that this procedure could be adapted to qualitative situations, in a wide range of subjects. For example, the preamble and target answers might be:

Napoleon invaded Russia in 1812. He was already ruler of most of Europe, though the offshore island of Britain remained unconquered and the Spanish peninsula was unpacified.

Answer:  The British Fleet dominated the seas.
Answer:  Napoleon tricked King Ferdinand into abdicating and replaced him with his own brother.

The wide range of questions that students might create should reveal more of their understanding than would a convergent response to a question written by the teacher.

### Strategy 4: Ask for Questions about Puzzling Points

The general form of this focussing strategy is to ask students to write questions about aspects of what they are learning which are puzzling to them. It is obviously related to the first of our five focussing strategies (questions of given structure such as 'What if . . .?').

The context of our first example is a science class of 15-year-olds who had completed a unit called 'Microscopes' and were now studying 'Cells'. The teacher formed the class into small groups, with each group to produce a single response to two tasks: (a) what the students knew about cells; (b) questions about cells that the students would like answered. As a starting point to the second task the teacher handed

## GROUP: C

- They grow and reproduce
- Plant cells hold the plant up
- There are plant and animal cells
- All cells are small
- Plant cells have got thick walls
- Cells can be stained
- They have a nucleus
- Cells are made up of different components
- They are in all living things
- Different shapes and sizes
- That cells die
- Cells hold us together

*Questions*

1   What happens to them when they die? Do they shrivel, decompose, etc.
2   Are they all the same colour?
3   How do cells get from one place to another? i.e., if someone touches another person, are they transmitted?
4   When a person (living thing) dies, what happens to the cells?
5   How many times can one cell break (multiply) or grow?
6   If cells have a constant supply of food do they live eternally?
7   If all living things are made of cells, is bacteria made up of cells or is it in cells?
8   Is hair dead cells or made up of cells?
9   What are cells made up of?
10  Have animal cells got thin walls or no walls at all?
     What is the diameter of an average animal cell?

## GROUP: E

- Two kinds: Animal, Plant
- Cells need food to survive
- They need nourishment
- Cells are in all parts of the body

*Questions*

1   Do teeth and bones have cells?
2   If blood renews itself every 3 weeks, do cells do so as well?
3   How does the body expel dead cells?
4   Is there a part of the body which produces cells?
5   How many cells are in a normal adult person?
6   If there is one nucleus in a cell, when the cell divides does the nucleus do so as well?
7   If bacteria eat each other, do cells do so too?
8   If plant cells are similar in size and shape, and neither is stronger, how do they eat each other?
9   If bacteria invades both plant and animal cells, which can fight it off more easily?
10  Do all bacteria thrive and breed in the same environment?

*Figure 10.8:   Student questions in response to the focus 'What questions about cells would you like answered?' (from Baird and Mitchell, 1986, p. 67)*

out a sheet on which were some questions which had already been raised by students individually or in whole class discussions. The products emerging from two groups are shown in Figure 10.8. It is also important in considering these questions to note that the teacher told the students before beginning the tasks that the questions they

- Who enforces civil law?
- Who made law? Why do we have to obey it?
- Who was the first country to make a law?
- If someone is out on bail in another state and breaks a law in Victoria, what happens?
- What happens when you vote twice?
- Why can girls marry (legally) earlier than boys?
- If someone throws something over your fence and you get hit, what will the charges be?
- If there was a gang fight and one was killed, who would be responsible?

*Figure 10.9:* *'Thinking questions' produced by 15-year-olds (from Baird and Mitchell, 1986, p. 201)*

produced would both be assessed and used to structure further class work. Again the most interesting feature we see in these questions is the great diversity in terms of intellectual demand.

A similar strategy is to ask for 'thinking questions', always supposing that students have an appropriate understanding of that term. Students in a parallel class to those whose questions are shown in Figure 10.1, 15-year-olds studying basic legal issues, were asked to write two thinking questions which went beyond the scope of classwork but which were related to the topic. Figure 10.9 shows a selection of responses.

We have used this strategy to good effect with adults also, in particular with science graduates in a pre-service teacher education program when teaching them about fundamental concepts of science. This is the context where it might seem the strategy is least likely to be successful, as the concepts being taught are ideas which the graduates all feel they should have understood years before (but which they very rarely do understand at all well). As one example we give some questions written by these pre-service science teachers during the teaching of fundamental concepts of electricity, in response to the task 'Write down any questions relating to today's session which are still puzzling you'. Common responses included questions of the following forms: How do, and how fast do, electrons move around a wire in an electric current? If electric current doesn't get used up, what does? Why does a light bulb get so hot if it is supposed to be giving off light not heat? Why can you recharge some batteries and not others? One motivation for using this strategy in this context is to shape the direction of subsequent classes.

*Strategy 5: Set Achievement Questions for a Section of Work*

This is in many ways the most demanding of our five suggested focussing strategies. The essence of the approach is to have students

167

undertake the same sorts of reviewing and thinking as you are involved in when you construct a test on some section of work you
have taught. At first sight it appears much more suited to mature
students. Indeed one of us was a student in a post-graduate course on
educational measurement for which 50 per cent of the assessment was
based on questions the students wrote which could be used to assess
achievement in the course we had just completed. The same approach
can, however, be used with much younger students.

The task shown in Figure 10.10 was one of three which made up
an assignment done by 14-year-olds which was used to grade their
performance after studying a novel.

Setting such tasks is, in itself, very simple. The same structure as
in Figure 10.10, 'Write X questions which would test a person's
understanding of Y', could be applied to any topic or subject. It is,
however, much more demanding to have students understand the
intent of the task. This is true for all of our strategies but most
strongly here. We return to this in the next section, on 'Introducing
Question Production to Students'.

## A General Comment on the Five Strategies

There are other ways of focussing students in their production of
questions. The strategies we have proposed fall into two broad
groups: strategies which aim to have students reflect on and try to link
and extend what they have learned ('What if ...?' and puzzling
questions); and strategies which try to put students into some sort of
imitation of the role usually adopted by those assessing student progress (write questions based on a given stimulus, write questions for a
given answer, write assessment questions). Other strategies for each
of these two broad groups of approaches surely exist.

## Introducing Question Production to Students

The common experience of teachers is that the first attempt at question production strategies with a group of students results in a large
proportion of purely factual questions. This is not surprising. Closed
questions, that is those with a single, unambiguous answer, are common in most classrooms, whether going from teacher to students or
students to teacher, while open and imaginative questions that require
reflection and understanding, both to frame and to answer, are rare.

1   *Understanding the Book*
Make up 10 questions which would test a person's understanding of the book.

Think about the setting, the characters, the character's actions, etc.

Try to include all the main events and happenings in your questions. You may need one question for every 2 or 3 chapters.

(Test these questions on a friend before handing in.)

Figure 10.10:   *Producing questions which could be used for assessing achievement (from Baird and Mitchell, 1986, p. 114)*

The latter are more valuable as indicators of understanding, but require students to adopt an unfamiliar role. Of course that is true of other techniques described in this book, but for them students usually have a stronger sense of the nature of the product. Students need guidance on the purpose of question production and on the sorts of questions that will be valued.

Time and experience, with feedback on the quality of their efforts, may give students an appreciation that matches your own of the purpose of the task and what is expected of them. In introducing question production, encourage the students to make an attempt, discuss with them their efforts, then have them try again.

One way to begin is to ask what the students believe they know about the topic before asking them to generate questions. This preceded the questions in the examples of Figures 10.1 and 10.8. When students set out what they know they have a clearer base for generating questions. Another approach is shown in Figure 10.11. This was an early use of question production in an English class of 12-year-olds. Here the teacher has both described the general nature of the question forms she is asking students to produce ('. . . how could things have turned out differently?') and given an example which students were required to answer. In later use of question production tasks the teacher gave less structure (and still received products of widely differing quality).

Discussion of responses, which is particularly important in the first few occurrences of question production, can lead to useful analyses of the nature of 'better' and 'not so good' products. Figure 10.12 shows an example of this, partly provided by the teacher and partly generated by the 14-year-old students who completed the task shown in Figure 10.10. This set of criteria for judging questions was then used by students in framing the achievement questions of Figure 10.10.

Another example comes from history classes with 14- and 15-year-olds. The students saw a videotape relevant to the topic for

*Think about what happened in the story and ask yourself how things could have turned out differently.*

What would have happened if John had never been left on his own for the day?

_____
_____
_____
_____

*Now it's your turn . . .*

What would have happened if _____
_____
_____ ?

How would things have been different if _____
_____
_____ ?

What do you think _____
_____
_____ ?

*Figure 10.11:  An early, more structured question production task based on a novel read by 12-year-olds (from Baird and Mitchell, 1986, p. 133)*

study. They were told that these questions would be assessed. They were also allowed to watch the video again if they wanted (some chose to watch it three times). The teacher collated the questions before the next class. Most were factual, some were thinking questions. The teacher used relevant examples to discuss differences and establish an idea of what thinking questions were. Students were then set the task of writing more thinking questions about the video, and so gradually came to understand the nature and purpose of this more demanding form of question.

Few students spontaneously ask high quality thinking questions. Nor do many acquire the skill easily. If you value the sorts of learning required by question production then you must devote sufficient class time to allow students to see the nature and purpose of this new student role. Failure to do this will very likely result in factual question production and frustration with this form of task. In our experience, though, such an expenditure of time is dramatically repaid by the enhanced learning that follows, as well as by the insights provided of the students' understanding.

**WRITING GOOD QUESTIONS**

*FACT QUESTIONS*

1  Your question can usually be answered in one or two words.
2  The answer is on a certain page in the book or notes.
3  The answer is either right or wrong.
4  The question usually starts with What, Where or When.

*PARTLY FACT, PARTLY THINKING QUESTIONS*

1  Your question usually requires a sentence or two answer.
2  The answer is not on any one page in the book or notes but, if you've understood the work you'll know it.
3  The answer will be right if explained well and you've understood the work, but could be wrong.
4  The question often starts with How.

*THINKING QUESTIONS*

1  Your question usually requires a paragraph answer.
2  The answer is not provided by the book or notes.
3  The answer will always be right if it makes sense according to the book or notes and is explained well.
4  The question often starts with Why or What if.

*Figure 10.12:   Criteria generated with and used by 14-year-old students to judge the quality of their question production (from Baird and Mitchell, 1986, p. 115)*

## Variations and Extensions

### 1   Call for Different Forms of Question

All of the examples given so far in this chapter have been of questions of the form teachers commonly ask. You could also ask students to generate questions in the forms of the less usual techniques that we have described in other chapters. Thus you could ask them to set concept mapping tasks, or relational diagrams, fortune lines and so forth.

This variation cannot be applied to all five of the strategies we suggested for question production. The first strategy, of asking for questions that begin in a particular form, assumes conventional questions, while to use other than conventional questioning to respond to 'What is puzzling me?' is to be unhelpfully complex. The third of our strategies (given an answer and ask for a question) may be appropriate for an alternative form such as fortune lines, but not for concept maps and relational diagrams. The remaining strategies (provide a stimulus and ask for student-generated questions, set achievement questions) can certainly be used with any of the other forms of probing which we described in this book.

### 2 *Have Students Answer the Questions Which Are Produced*

This can be either their own questions or those from others in the class. Again it is an extension more suited to some forms of question production strategies than others. There are clear problems with asking students to generate questions about things that puzzle them and then immediately requiring that these be answered. (Although a somewhat different approach to requiring answers to these particular questions can be extremely valuable as a classroom strategy. We discuss this in the later section on uses in teaching.)

One successful approach, intermediate between students answering their own questions or answering those from another student, is to group students. It is often possible to group together students who have generated similar questions. Then the group is given the task of selecting and answering one of these similar questions.

### 3 *Extend 2 by Having Students Assess Answers to Produced Questions*

We suggested in an earlier section of this chapter that one way to consider the purposes of having students generate questions is in terms of trying to imitate the thinking required of teachers when they generate demanding questions. The extension we suggest here is the logical one of having students imitate teachers in ways which will reveal student understanding.

It is common for teachers to react to suggestions that students assess themselves or classmates with beliefs that students will be very liberal in their assessments. In our considerable experience of using this strategy, and in the experience of teachers with whom we have worked, this is rarely so. It is more common for students to be unreasonably hard in their assessments, including self assessments.

### What the Procedure Reveals

It is less easy to be specific about what question production reveals of understanding than it is for most of the other techniques we describe, because what is revealed varies with the focussing strategy which is used and with the nature of the topic. Consider, for example, the fifth of our focussing strategies: writing questions which could be used to assess someone's understanding of a section of work. If the section of work is a novel, as in the example shown in Figure 10.10, then the task is aimed at exploring student understanding of extensive communications. On the other hand, if the section of work is an overarching concept such as Energy in a science course, then it is aspects of understanding of a concept which are being revealed.

A further complication for considering what the procedure reveals is that the nature of the product that is the outcome of the task is more likely to vary across students for question production than for our other probes. There is after all less of a predetermining structure here than for the other procedures.

Even with this general difficulty with what is revealed, a more specific comment is possible for two of our five focussing strategies. In particular, questions of particular structure and questions about things that are puzzling will likely involve students in restructuring, extending and linking their ideas. This will lead to revealing aspects of the understanding of the concepts about which the questions were to be asked.

## Scoring of Question Production

If, for summative assessment, you want to score the questions students produce, the students must understand your expectations. Consider a circumstance where this is not so, and students have been given the first task shown in Figure 10.7: Write a question which could have as an answer 'Because Brazil is not surrounded by water'. If students do not understand that 'fact' questions are to be less valued than 'thinking' questions, then you will have no grounds for distinguishing between 'Why is Brazil not called an island?' and 'Why can the Amazon river flow across the whole width of Brazil?'

If we assume that the students understand the purpose of the task, then scoring can readily be related to this purpose. It is a more obvious process for three of our suggested focussing strategies: questions based on a given stimulus, questions based on a given answer, and achievement questions for a segment of classroom work. The analogy of assessment of essays and extended writing which we used in discussing scoring of concept maps is relevant here. Your purposes may well allow you to employ a mark allocation scheme that lists

*One Mark Questions:*

- Is friction a force like gravity?
    (Yes/No question)
- Why doesn't the chair push up when only a little weight is on it?
    (Similar to our notes)

*Two Mark Questions:*

- Seeing there is no gravity under water why do things, e.g., rocks, fall to the sea bed?
    (New situation, incorrect assumption)
- How can there be a reaction force on the ground when you are walking?
    (Slightly new situation, is readily answerable from work so far)
- If gravity is all over the earth how come when you are under water you go up?
- What do forces and movement have in common, i.e., WHY did you call the unit this?

*Three Mark Questions:*

- We can move around freely. Why do we always fall down so quickly?
    Is there just enough gravity to hold us down?
    (This calls for a new, different application for our model)
- Is there still gravity in a room with no air? What would you have to do to get rid of gravity?
    Can you do it?
- Why does the earth go round the sun and not stay still? What makes it float? Why doesn't
    it fall?
    (Considerable imagination shown here)

Figure 10.13:   An example of assessment of puzzling questions (teacher comments in
parentheses)

issues and ideas that you judge must be included in the questions. This scheme might reward questions that are central to the topic, require high quality thinking, expressed clearly, and are of appropriate level of difficulty. In other circumstances you may use a more global approach to evaluation of students' efforts.

When students are uncertain of the value of asking questions, scoring of puzzling questions and questions of particular linguistic form can make them feel insecure and inhibit them from taking part. If, however, they comprehend that asking questions demonstrates understanding and promotes better learning, scoring might not do much harm. Knowing that their questions would be scored does not seem to have inhibited the 15-year-olds whose questions, with scores and teacher's comments, appear in Figure 10.13. The students had to write questions that puzzled them about force and motion. They had done this sort of task before, and most appeared to accept the value of its purpose.

## Using Question Production in Teaching

Earlier in this chapter we mentioned two general uses of question production. One is the structuring of further work on a topic. Questions that students see as puzzling are particularly appropriate for this purpose. The second use is to have students answer, either individually or in groups, questions that they or others have generated.

Questions which are puzzling may appear inappropriate for subsequent student answering, since to be puzzling they cannot be answered by the students. Puzzling questions can, however, be the basis for subsequent student research in the library or laboratory. There is strong motivation in this, for students are keener to answer their own questions than the teacher's. This use combines structuring further work and having students answer questions. Such an approach may seem to make it difficult for the teacher to maintain the intended curriculum, but in our experience it is common for puzzling questions to embrace topics that the teacher intended to reach sooner or later.

One of our strategies for focussing student question production was to require the writing of achievement questions for a section of work. We have worked with some high school teachers who have taken this to its obvious conclusion and have had students set questions for their own achievement tests. Experience suggests this is best done in small groups, with the teacher selecting the final test from the questions produced by each group. On the first occasion that students do this it is helpful to discuss with them some necessary attributes of a test that they would see as fair: coverage of all the work; a variety of question types, not solely knowledge recall; able to be marked reliably. The real purpose is the learning that the task fosters. This can involve students in considerable thought about the relative importance of sections of the work.

As with any strategy, over-use of this approach can result in student dislike of the task, and trivial and ritualized responses.

Other probes require students to respond in a more-or-less focussed way to a task controlled by the teacher. Question asking is more open, and throws more responsibility on to the student. This enables it, when attempted conscientiously, to make the student aware of personal uncertainty about the topic. Of course all probes can do that, but question asking is particularly powerful in bringing home to individuals the quality of their understanding.

## Further Reading

BAIRD, J.R. and MITCHELL, I.J. (1986) *Improving the Quality of Teaching and Learning: An Australian Case-Study — The Peel Project*, Melbourne: Monash University.

We took a number of the examples in this chapter from this set of accounts by teachers of their own teaching. It is the only example of which we are aware of such descriptions of approaches to question asking.

*Chapter 11*

# Validity and Reliability

If you were asked to describe your house, you could give a simple answer ('It is small') or you could start on a lengthy description, listing its area, number of rooms and their types, number of storeys, mode of construction, colour, direction it faces, location, and so forth. Some of the properties you list may have a numerical value, others will be qualitative descriptions. The more properties you list, presumably the more informative the description. So it is with understanding. Like a house, understanding is multi-dimensional. It depends on how much you know, what sorts of things you know, how well integrated they are, your commitment to this knowledge, and so on. Thus, just as your house cannot be described completely by a single measure, nor can understanding. The more measures you take, the more complete the assessment.

Appreciation of the complexity of understanding has certain consequences. One, which is an obvious theme of this book, is that the wider the range of measures used to probe understanding, the better the assessment. Even if the final purpose of the assessment is to arrive at a single decision, such as whether the person has a good enough understanding to be given a pass in a course or to be allowed to move on to further study, that decision will be sounder if based on diverse measures than on a limited set.

## Validity

Validity is the term for how appropriate a judgement (or score) is of whatever it purports to measure. Thus we can consider whether a score on a multiple choice test, say, is a valid assessment of intelligence. We can argue whether scholastic aptitude tests are more valid

177

than tests of subject matter knowledge as measures of ability to succeed in a university course. It is relatively easy to judge the validity of tests of limited, one-dimensional skills such as the ability to add single-digit numbers. With such narrowly-defined skills we expect high agreement between judges of whether a test is a valid measure, and we would also expect that tests people devise for them would be closely similar. But with more complex or multi-dimensional attributes such as understanding, that are much more difficult to define, it is not so easy to determine what constitutes a valid test. We would expect greater divergence between tests that different people construct, and greater disagreement about the validity of a measure. Our point is that such divergences and disagreements are not a matter for concern. Rather, for a complex notion like understanding, they are to be welcomed. Our description in Chapter 1 of different targets of understanding is just one example of the need for a variety of approaches.

Texts on the theory of measurement describe an aspect of validity known as content validity — whether the test samples adequately the range of subject matter or objectives that it is supposed to assess. Behind our advocacy of diverse probes of understanding is concern for what we will term *mode validity* — whether the assessment samples adequately the range of ways of expressing or demonstrating understanding. Current assessment usually has low mode validity.

Measurement texts rarely, if ever, note that there is a reciprocal interaction between objectives and validity of measurement. Most restrict their discussion to the point that the more of the facets of a construct, such as understanding of a topic or dimensions of a house, that the assessment covers, the more valid it is. But assessment affects objectives, so that a narrow measure of a construct can gradually alter our perception of it. An instance is the way in which the notion of intelligence is shaped by the tests used to determine IQ. As the concept itself is narrowed by the tests, so the narrow tests appear to be more valid measures of the concept. The longer this goes on, the more comfortable the fit between the concept and the test. What we must appreciate is that the price of that comfort may be a loss of the original richness of meaning of the concept. Attention to mode validity is one way of maintaining that richness of meaning.

Richness of meaning of understanding is important in education. The meaning people give to understanding affects the way they teach things and how they learn them. More bluntly, the test determines how things will be taught and learned. This is true even for our analogy of the house. When houses in Britain were assessed for taxes by their number of windows, people built houses with fewer windows. Measuring understanding in only one or two ways, as is in fact common practice, similarly leads to narrowness of teaching and learning. An increase in methods of probing understanding will broaden teaching methods and learning styles.

Forms of assessment shape students' views of subjects. Some years ago, when one of us was teaching in a high school, a colleague set a history test that included the question 'Australian aboriginals are ___'. One student wrote 'black', which the teacher marked as wrong. The required answer was 'nomads', which the teacher justified on the grounds that it was what was in the students' notes. The teacher's action, and the nature of the test, conveyed to the students a view that history is a convergent, conforming subject in which there are specific answers and no room for opinion. The student who wrote 'black' had so far adopted this view he was not aggrieved by the treatment his answer received. As far as he was concerned, history comprised isolated arbitrary facts, and was boring and irrelevant. He could not conceive of any other attribute for the discipline. His low motivation for history followed from the nature of the testing he experienced in it.

Diverse methods of assessment improve the quality of learning in two ways. First, they promote greater awareness by students of the quality of their learning. Concept maps, for instance, show people whether they have perceived links between topics. They also show people that there is a need to form links, a need that research (and the experience of teachers) has shown is only too often overlooked. Relational diagrams make people aware of the fuzziness of their understandings of specific terms, and can change their learning styles so that they strive for sharper apprehensions. Second, diverse methods show students that subjects involve a range of learning outcomes and are far more interesting in consequence. They show that history is not just facts, that mathematics is not just repetitive algorithms. Sensible application of a range of probes of understanding makes learning more enjoyable and purposeful.

## Understanding and Controlling Personal Learning

Greater awareness of the quality of one's own learning leads to greater control over it. Teachers and researchers are concerned that many students are passive in learning. Few question what they are told or reflect on its implications; few think about the relevance of what they are learning for their present and future lives; few go beyond the bounds of tasks set by the teacher in order to find out more for themselves. This poverty of learning is at best dimly recognised, so only rarely is anything done about it. Introduction of diverse probes of understanding is one key step in breaking this pattern of comfortable mediocrity.

## Further Alternative Assessment Approaches

It is one thing to appreciate the value of diverse probes, it is another to put them into practice. In each chapter we included a section on introducing the method to students, since we are conscious that people have to learn how to respond to each new procedure. Students will rarely perform well instantly with a new style of test. The teacher, too, has to learn through experience how to get the most out of each procedure. No doubt all that is obvious, but what is less readily appreciated is that teachers have to be wary of over-use of a method once it has been learned.

If any form of assessment is used too frequently, students can learn to respond automatically. Consequently the assessment might no longer measure quite what you want it to. Its validity lessens. People appreciate that this is so for well-known forms such as multiple choice tests. If we have two students with equal understanding, the one who is familiar with multiple choice tests will get an inflated score because of skills acquired through experience of ruling out distractors, willingness to guess, or better management of time. There is nothing wrong with having such skills, but they are not part of the understanding that the test is intended to measure. We have observed this problem with concept maps and interviews. Experience shows students what sort of concept map is valued — one with lots of cross-links and complex structure. They will then work to present such a map, whatever their state of understanding. The implication is that it is best to use a range of methods that is wide enough to prevent over-familiarity. Thus there has to be a balance between so rapid an introduction of new probes that students never become familiar with any and so static a situation that the methods become stale.

In this book we have described a number of probes of understanding so that teachers will have a range to choose from. This set is not presented as an exhaustive list, for many other forms may exist or yet be invented.

One possibility is the adaptation from the concept map of the

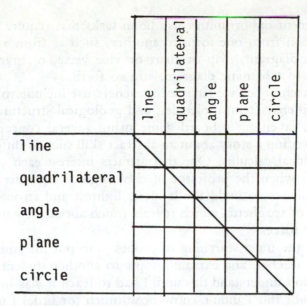

Figure 11.1:   A concept chart

concept chart. Here the selected concepts are placed along the top and down one side of a grid, as shown in Figure 11.1. The students' task is to write the relation between each pair of concepts in the appropriate cell.

Written text offers useful possibilities. Sub-headings can be removed from a passage, and students then have to supply appropriate ones. In this task there is no need to tell students the location of the original sub-headings. Another approach is to jumble the paragraphs of a passage and ask students to re-order them appropriately. You can extend this by including diagrams from the original text, with captions removed, which the students have to insert at appropriate spots and provide new captions. In both of these text examples, a further extension is to require students to explain their answers. Not only does this explanation reveal more of the understanding, it also copes with the fact that more than one answer may be suitable.

The two text tasks assess the links that students see between concepts or ideas. A more direct approach is to ask students to describe the links between material on two selected, widely separated pages. Analogies also offer useful possibilities for probing links. An imaginative instance, that we saw recently in a class of 14-year-olds, called for the students to describe the similarities and differences of Norse sagas and television soap operas.

Assessment opportunities also lie in tasks that require translation of information from one form to another, such as from a paragraph of text to a diagram, map or chart or vice versa, or graph to text, photograph to schematic diagram, and so forth.

Other techniques we have seen teachers use include role playing, for historical characters, molecules, and geological structures; simulation games; inventing a board game using several concepts from a topic; and writing a story about an abstract skill such as differentiating in mathematical calculus. One that attracts interest each year at our university is when the professor of civil engineering runs a competition for students to build the longest, lightest and strongest bridge from sticks of spaghetti, which reveals much about their understanding of static forces.

One of the most searching of probes is to put the student in the place of the teacher, and explain a topic to another student. The trite saying 'I didn't understand this until I had to teach it' has another side: 'Until I taught this I didn't know how much (or little) I understood about it.'

No doubt each teacher could add further innovatory probes.

## Reliability

As well as validity, reliability is another key notion in measurement. Reliability refers to the consistency of the judgement that follows from use of a test. If the students did the test again, would they score the same? That is test-retest reliability. If the test were split into two parts, would a person's performance on each half lead to the same judgement? That is internal consistency. If the responses were scored by different judges, would they arrive at the same assessments? That is reader reliability. Of course reliability is an important property of a probe, though one must not forget that a test can be reliable but not valid.

Although high reliability is an advantage, it is only one factor to consider in evaluating a method of testing. Excessive emphasis on reliability can reduce the mode validity of assessment. One of the reasons for the popularity of multiple choice questions, which reached a peak in the 1950s and 1960s, was their high reliability. They tended to replace essays in many subject examinations, especially in the sciences, in part because essays were notorious for low reader reliability (ease of marking and high subject content validity were other factors). Much later, concern became widespread that excessive re-liance on multiple choice tests excluded evaluation of important object-ives such as ability to explain or to construct a reasoned argument. High reliability was achieved at the cost of validity.

There is a further point to note about high reliability. While internal consistency and reader reliability should always exercise the minds of those who assess, we see test–retest reliability differently because of our interest in the influence that assessment has on the quality of learning. People learn from tests. An obvious characteristic, though one neglected by measurement theorists, of an assessment with high test–retest reliability is that undergoing it did not change the students much. A high test–retest reliability carries the assumption that the student should learn little from the task. Though it is possible to devise tests like that, we do not see it as desirable. The better the assessment reveals the student's understanding, the more likely the student will learn something — and hence the greater the discrepancy between first and second test performance. Since a key purpose of this book is to propagate practices that cause students to rethink, to make new links, to ask questions — in short, to learn — we value test–retest reliability less than other forms of reliability. Indeed, low test–retest reliability may be welcomed if it results from the intellectual demand of the assessment stimulating deeper learning.

The probes of understanding that we have described vary in the ease with which they can be made reliable. Relational diagrams should have good reader reliability, but concept maps and interviews have greater subjectivity in their interpretation and perhaps less stability — how the person feels, for instance, is more likely to affect performance on a concept map or in an interview than it is on doing a relational diagram. Lower innate internal consistency or reader reliability of some probes does not make them any less valuable than does the lower reliability of essays make them less valuable than multiple choice tests. We should try to make each probe as reliable as possible, for instance by ensuring that respondents are familiar with it and by using standard procedures, but we should not rule out a probe solely because it is less reliable than other forms of test.

A major theme of our book is that validity of assessment of understanding increases with the range of appropriate probes that is used. That theme is coupled with another, that better assessment of understanding will lead to better teaching and learning. Better teaching and learning are fine objectives. Time spent in school should be productive. There is no reason why it should not be enjoyable as well. As things stand, students and teachers rarely rate tests as fun, perhaps because they are so limited and predictable. A greater variety of probes of understanding makes testing more interesting as well as more useful. We are confident that teachers who use the techniques described in this book will find it so, and their students will too.

# References

ANDERSSON, B. and KÄRRQVIST, C. (1979) *Elektriska Kretsar*, Elevperspectiv 2, Götheborg, Sweden: Department of Educational Research, University of Götheborg.

AUSUBEL, D.P. (1963) *The Psychology of Meaningful Verbal Learning*, New York: Grune & Stratton.

AUSUBEL, D.P. (1968) *Educational Psychology: A Cognitive View*, New York: Holt, Rinehart & Winston.

BAIRD, J.R. and MITCHELL, I.J. (Eds) (1986) *Improving the Quality of Teaching and Learning: An Australian Case Study — The Peel Project*, Melbourne: Monash University.

BARNES, D.R. (1976) *From Communication to Curriculum*, Harmondsworth, England: Penguin Books.

BELL, B.F. (1981) 'When is an animal, not an animal?', *Journal of Biological Education*, **15**, pp. 213–18.

BLOOM, B.S. (Ed.) (1956) *Taxonomy of Educational Objectives Handbook 1: Cognitive Domain*, New York: Longmans, Green & Co.

BROWN, A.L. (1980) 'Metacognitive development and reading', in SPIRO, R.J. *et al.* (Eds) *Theoretical Issues in Reading Comprehension: Perspectives from Cognitive Psychology, Linguistics, Artificial Intelligence, and Education*, Hillsdale, N.J: Erlbaum.

BRUMBY, M. (1982) 'Medical students' perception of science', *Research in Science Education*, **12**, pp. 107–14.

BUROS, O.K. (Ed.) (1938) *The Nineteen Thirty-Eight Mental Measurements Yearbook of the School of Education, Rutgers University*, New Brunswick, N.J: Rutgers University Press.

CHAMBERS, D.W. (1983) 'Stereotypic images of the scientist: The draw-a-scientist test', *Science Education*, **67**, pp. 255–65.

DEESE, J. (1962) 'On the structure of associative meaning', *Psychological Review*, **69**, pp. 161–75.

DRIVER, R. (1983) *The Pupil as Scientist*? Milton Keynes: Open University Press.

ERICKSON, G.L. (1979) 'Children's conceptions of heat and temperature', *Science Education*, **63**, pp. 221–30.

FISHER, K.M., FALETTI, J., PATTERSON, H., THORNTON, R., LIPSON, J. and SPRING, C. (1990) 'Computer-based concept mapping: Sem-Net software, a tool for describing knowledge networks', *Journal of College Science Teaching*, **19**, pp. 347–52.

FLANDERS, N.A. (1970) *Analyzing Teaching Behavior*, Reading, Mass: Addison-Wesley.

FREDETTE, N. and LOCHHEAD, J. (1980) 'Student conceptions of simple circuits', *The Physics Teacher*, **18**, pp. 194–8.

GAGNÉ, R.M. (1965) *The Conditions of Learning* (1st ed.), New York: Holt, Rinehart & Winston.

GAGNÉ, R.M. and WHITE, R.T. (1978) 'Memory structures and learning outcomes', *Review of Educational Research*, **48**, pp. 187–222.

GARSKOFF, B.E. and HOUSTON, J.P. (1963) 'Measurement of verbal relatedness: An idiographic approach', *Psychological Review*, **70**, pp. 277–88.

GILBERT, J.K., WATTS, D.M. and OSBORNE, R.J. (1985) 'Eliciting student views using an interview-about-instances technique', in WEST, L.H.T. and PINES, A.L. (Eds) *Cognitive Structure and Conceptual Change*, Orlando, Florida: Academic Press.

GRUBER, H.E. and VONECHE, J.J. (Eds) (1977) *The Essential Piaget*, London: Routledge & Kegan Paul.

GUNSTONE, R.F. (1980) *Structural Outcomes of Physics Instruction*, Unpublished Ph.D. thesis, Melbourne, Monash University.

GUNSTONE, R.F. and CHAMPAGNE, A.B. (1990) 'Promoting conceptual change in the laboratory', in HEGARTY-HAZEL, E. (Ed.) *The Student Laboratory and the Science Curriculum*, London: Routledge.

GUNSTONE, R.F., MITCHELL, I.J. and THE MONASH CHILDREN'S SCIENCE GROUP (1988) 'Two teaching strategies for considering children's science', In *The Yearbook of the International Council of Associations of Science Education*, pp. 1–12.

GUNSTONE, R.F. and WHITE, R.T. (1981) 'Understanding of gravity', *Science Education*, **65**, pp. 291–9.

GUNSTONE, R.F. and WHITE, R.T. (1983) 'Testing and teaching with Venn diagrams', *Australian Science Teachers Journal*, **29**, 3, pp. 63–4.

GUNSTONE, R.F. and WHITE, R.T. (1986) 'Assessing understanding by means of Venn diagrams', *Science Education*, **70**, pp. 151–8.

HOLT, J. (1967) *How Children Fail*, New York, Pitman.

INHELDER, B. and PIAGET, J. (1958) *The Growth of Logical Thinking from Childhood to Adolescence: An Essay on the Construction of Formal Operational Structures* (A. Parsons and S. Milgram, *Trans.*), New York: Basic Books. (Original work published 1955.)

JOHNSON, P.E. (1964) 'Associative meaning of concepts in physics', *Journal of Educational Psychology*, **55**, pp. 84–8.

JOHNSON, P.E. (1967) 'Some psychological aspects of subject–matter structure', *Journal of Educational Psychology*, **58**, pp. 75–83.

JOHNSON, P.E. (1969) 'On the communication of concepts in science', *Journal of Educational Psychology*, **60**, pp. 32–40.

KINNEAR, J., GLEESON, D. and COMERFORD, C. (1985) 'Use of concept maps in assessing the value of a computer-based activity in biology', *Research in Science Education*, **15**, pp. 103–11.

KOESTLER, A. (1964) *The Act of Creation*, London: Hutchinson.

MEAD, M. and METRAUX, R. (1957) 'The image of the scientist among high school students: A pilot study', *Science*, **126**, pp. 384–90.

MITCHELL, J. (1986) in BAIRD, J.R. and MITCHELL, I.J. (Eds), *Improving the Quality of Teaching and Learning: An Australian Case Study — The Peel Project*, Melbourne: Monash University.

NEUREITHER, B. (1990) 'Misconceptions — the tip of the iceberg', *IRT Communication Quarterly*, **12**, 3, p. 2.

NOVAK, J.D. and GOWIN, D.B. (1984) *Learning How to Learn*, Cambridge: Cambridge University Press.

NOVICK, S. and NUSSBAUM, J. (1978) 'Junior high school pupils' understanding of the particulate nature of matter: An interview study', *Science Education*, **62**, pp. 273–81.

NUSSBAUM, J. (1979) 'Children's conceptions of the Earth as a cosmic body: A cross age study', *Science Education*, **63**, pp. 83–93.

NUSSBAUM, J. and NOVAK, J.D. (1976) 'An assessment of children's concepts of the earth utilizing structured interviews', *Science Education*, **60**, pp. 535–50.

OSBORNE, R.J. (1980) *Electric Current*, Paper No. 25, Learning in Science Project, New Zealand: University of Waikato.

OSBORNE, R.J. and FREYBERG, P. (1985) *Learning in Science: The Implications of Children's Science*, Auckland: Heinemann.

OSBORNE, R.J. and GILBERT, J.K. (1980) 'A method for investigating concept understanding in science', *European Journal of Science Education*, **2**, pp. 311–21.

PARIS, S.G., SAARNIO, D.A. and CROSS, D.R. (1986) 'A metacognitive curriculum to promote children's reading and learning', *Australian Journal of Psychology*, **38**, pp. 107–23.

PIAGET, J. (1969) *The Child's Conception of Physical Causality*, (M.

Gabain *Trans*.), Totowa, New Jersey: Littlefield Adams. (Original work published 1927.)

PIAGET, J. (1969) *The Child's Conception of Time*, (A.J. Pomerans, *Trans*.), London: Routledge and Kegan Paul. (Original work published 1946.)

PIAGET, J. (1970) *The Child's Conception of Movement and Speed*, (G.E.T. Holloway and M.J. Mackenzie, *Trans*.), London: Routledge and Kegan Paul. (Original work published 1946.)

PINES, A.L., NOVAK, J.D., POSNER, G.J. and VAN KIRK, J. (1978) *The Clinical Interview: A Method for Evaluating Cognitive Structure*, Ithaca, N.Y: Cornell University Department of Education Curriculum Series Report No. 6.

POSNER, G.J., STRIKE, K.A., HEWSON, P.W. and GERTZOG, W.A. (1982) 'Accommodation of a scientific conception: Toward a theory of conceptual change', *Science Education*, **66**, pp. 211–27.

PREECE, P.F.W. (1976) 'Mapping cognitive structure: A comparison of methods', *Journal of Educational Psychology*, **68**, pp. 1–8.

RUSH, L.N. (1988) *Fortune lines — A new probe of understanding in the humanities*. Unpublished Master of Educational Studies project, Melbourne, Monash University.

SCHANK, R.C. and ABELSON, R.P. (1977) *Scripts, Plans, Goals, and Understanding: An Inquiry into Human Knowledge Structures*, Hillsdale, N.J.: Erlbaum.

SHAVELSON, R.J. (1972) 'Some aspects of the correspondence between content structure and cognitive structure in physics instruction', *Journal of Educational Psychology*, **63**, pp. 225–34.

SHAVELSON, R.J. (1973) 'Learning from physics instruction', *Journal of Research in Science Teaching*, **10**, pp. 101–11.

SHAVELSON, R.J. (1974) 'Methods for examining representations of a subject–matter structure in a student's memory', *Journal of Research in Science Teaching*, **11**, pp. 231–49.

STEAD, B.F. and OSBORNE, R.J. (1980) 'Exploring science students' concepts of light', *Australian Science Teachers Journal*, **26**, 3, pp. 84–90.

STEAD, K.E. and OSBORNE, R.J. (1980) *Friction*, Paper No. 19, Learning in Science Project, New Zealand: University of Waikato.

STEAD, K.E. and OSBORNE, R.J. (1981) 'What is friction? — Some children's ideas', *Australian Science Teachers Journal*, **27**, 3, pp. 51–7.

STEWART, J. (1979) 'Content and cognitive structure: Critique of assessment and representation techniques used by science education researchers', *Science Education*, **63**, pp. 395–405.

SYMINGTON, D., BOUNDY, K., RADFORD, T. and WALTON, J. (1981) 'Children's drawings of natural phenomena', *Research in Science Education*, **11**, pp. 44–51.

TASKER, R. (1981) 'Children's views and classroom experiences', *Australian Science Teachers Journal*, **27**, 3, pp. 33–7.

TIBERGHIEN, A. and DELACOTE, G. (1976) 'Manipulation et représentations des circuits électriques simple par des enfants de 7 à 12 ans', *Revue Française de Pédagogie*, **34**, pp. 32–44.

TRAVERS, R.M.W. and RABINOWITZ, W. (1953) 'A drawing technique for studying certain outcomes of teacher education, Part II. A quantitative comparison of certain outcomes in two institutions', in TRAVERS, R.M.W., RABINOWITZ, W., PAGE, M.H., NEMO-VICHER, E. and VENTUR, P. *Exploratory Studies in Teacher Personality*, New York: City Colleges, Division of Teacher Education.

WHITE, R.T. (1988) *Learning Science*, Oxford, Blackwell.

WHITE, R.T. and GUNSTONE, R.F. (1980) 'Converting memory protocols to scores on several dimensions', *Australian Association for Research in Education Annual Conference Papers*, pp. 486–93.

WITTROCK, M.C. (1974) 'Learning as a generative process', *Educational Psychologist*, **11**, pp. 87–95.

# Index